When You
Can't Find God

Other Books by Linda Evans Shepherd

When You Don't Know What to Pray:
How to Talk to God about Anything
The Potluck Club Cookbook

The Potluck Club
The Potluck Club—Trouble's Brewing
The Potluck Club—Takes the Cake

The Potluck Catering Club Series
The Secret's in the Sauce
A Taste of Fame
Bake Until Golden

When You Can't Find God

How to IGNITE the POWER of HIS Presence

Linda Evans Shepherd

Revell

a division of Baker Publishing Group
Grand Rapids, Michigan

Published by Revell
a division of Baker Publishing Group
P.O. Box 6287, Grand Rapids, MI 49516-6287
www.revellbooks.com

Printed in the United States of America

Library of Congress Cataloging-in-Publication Data
Shepherd, Linda E., 1957–
    When you can't find God : how to ignite the power of his presence / Linda
Evans Shepherd.
        p.   cm.
    Includes bibliographical references.
    ISBN 978-0-8007-1978-4 (pbk.)
    1. Suffering—Religious aspects—Christianity. 2. Prayer—Christianity. I.
Title.
BV4909.S495 2011
242′.4—dc22   2011000138

11   12   13   14   15   16   17   7 6 5 4 3 2 1

I thank the Lord for trials because they have taught me how to see and trust him in the dark.

I especially thank my loving husband, Paul, and our children, Laura and Jim, who have shared this journey with me. I also thank my parents, who have always been an inspiration. Plus, kudos to my agent, Janet Kobobel Grant, my editor, Vicki Crumpton, and all my friends at Baker Publishing Group; I so appreciate you. I'm also sending a special thank-you to my prayer partners, Carole Whang Schutter, Rebekah Montgomery, and the entire AWSA prayer team. You helped pray me through the writing of this book.

I am so blessed that you are in my life.

Love,
Linda

Contents

For my readers, family, and friends—
"God is our refuge and strength,
an ever-present help in trouble." (Ps. 46:1)

1

When Difficulties Come

Comfort and prosperity have never enriched the world as much as adversity has.

—Billy Graham[1]

Promise Me a Pain-Free Life

Tracy clenched the steering wheel as she sped toward the airport in her tiny car. Her blue eyes reflected her misery. She asked, "What I want to know is this: will I always have emotional pain in my life?"

Her words were a continuation of a conversation we'd started earlier that weekend when she'd picked me up at the airport to take me to a women's conference. Along the miles, Tracy had described her childhood abuse and told me about her severe depression, for which she was under a doctor's care.

I answered, "I can tell you God loves you, but I can't promise that you'll live the rest of your life totally free of pain."

Tracy frowned and appeared to study the eighteen-wheelers rushing toward us in the opposite lane of the freeway. "You don't understand. I'm desperate to know that I won't always hurt."

I watched as she twitched both her gaze and steering wheel as if she were thinking of plunging our car across the dividing line to meet an approaching tanker.

Alarmed, I said, "Tracy, I wish I could promise you that you will never hurt again, but I can tell you there's hope. You can trust God, you really can."

The car rocked as the eighteen-wheeler rushed past us. Ahead I could see miles of big rigs, one following the other as they sped toward us.

Tracy swatted away a tear. "But I need to *know* that I won't have to live with my pain forever."

> The enemy knows God has a purpose and plan for your life. The enemy is the one who wants you to give up.

As she began to eye the next tanker, I wished I could simply say, "Say this magical prayer with me, Tracy, and all your troubles and pain will be gone forever."

Instead I said, "Tracy, God loves you. You can ask him for help. God *will* hear you."

"But I can't wait. I need help now or I might as well be dead."

I took in a deep breath. "But Scripture says, 'Anyone who is among the living has hope—even a live dog is better off than a dead lion!'"

Tracy stared at the trucks whizzing past. "I'd rather be that dead lion."

"But you can't give up on God, you *can't*. This may be the very moment of your breakthrough. The enemy knows God has a purpose and plan for your life. The enemy is the one who wants you to give up."

This truth seemed to calm her, and as she continued to drive, I quietly assured her of God's love and purpose for her life. When Tracy pulled in front of my airline's drop-off, I hugged her and prayed with her, but I could see in her eyes that her pain persisted.

Are Pain and Trouble Even Biblical?

An hour later, as I sat on the plane winging my way back to Colorado, I considered and prayed for this young lady who had so desperately pleaded for a pain-free life. I also thought of my own pain. It had been twenty years since a violent car crash had hurled my baby, while still in her car seat, into the middle of the freeway. Though my child had finally returned to me from her year-long coma, I'd been heartbroken when she'd woken up with severe disabilities. Oh, I understood pain and difficulties—I'd wrestled with them then, and I still face circumstances today that bring me pain.

> So maybe we should consider this: if God's own Son didn't get through life without pain and difficulties, why do we expect to do so?

But Tracy and I, and maybe even you, aren't the only ones who have ever dealt with difficulties. Let me name a few biblical greats who endured their share of trouble and heartache. My greatly abbreviated list includes notables such as Adam and Eve, Noah, Abraham, Jacob, Job, Joseph, Moses, David, Elisha, Mary (the blessed one), the disciples, the sisters Mary and Martha, oh and let's see, even Jesus himself. (Well, at least we're in good company.)

Jesus? Well, yes, he suffered more than anyone. So maybe we should consider this: if God's own Son didn't get through life without pain and difficulties, why do we expect to do so?

I once heard a message by Dr. David Jeremiah on his radio program, *Turning Point*, where he explained that many people who come to Christ expect to leave their difficulties behind only to discover that their lives have become even more complicated.

Dr. Jeremiah explained, "God never told us that it would be easy. He never gave us any reason to believe that if we became children of God through faith in Jesus Christ that we would be without problems."[2]

> "Trouble is here. It is for a purpose. Use it for the purpose for which it was intended—to help you grow. Thank God for your troubles."—Dr. Norman Vincent Peale

Dr. Jeremiah speaks the truth. In fact, even the apostle James said, "Consider it pure joy, my brothers, whenever you face trials of many kinds, because you know that the testing of your faith develops perseverance" (James 1:2–3).

James understood the secret of how not only to survive pain and difficulties but to find strength and the resulting miracle, a transformed life.

I like how the late Dr. Norman Vincent Peale put it when he said, "Trouble is here. It is for a purpose. Use it for the purpose for which it was intended—to help you grow. Thank God for your troubles."[3]

Are you serious? Well, yes, as I'll soon explain, and I'll also explain how you can live not as a victim but as a victor as I help you discover how to find real joy and rest. But before we get started, I want to take you to the place where several biblical greats including Moses, Elisha, and the wandering Israelites not only met trouble but also met God.

The Mountain of God

I once flew over the mountainous desert where the Israelites had wandered for forty years. As I gazed down on the bleak landscape,

I saw it was dotted with drab brush and punctuated with pointed mountains that looked much like the pyramids. Although no one is sure which of these peaks is *the* Mount Horeb, we have a record of its colorful history.

For starters, we know that it was in this desert, between these desolate mountains, that a former prince of Egypt hid from his past by joining a wandering Midianite family. Back in Egypt, Prince Moses, a Hebrew himself, killed a man for striking a Hebrew slave. Being a wanted man, he fled from the scene of the crime and disappeared into the wilderness. He hid his clean-shaven face with a beard and dressed in the garb of a desert nomad as he tended a herd of sheep.

But it was in this desolate place, at the base of Mount Horeb, where Moses encountered God in a burning bush. It was here that Moses found redemption from his past and received a purpose that God himself would empower him to fulfill.

Perhaps you, too, are in a desolate place. If so, I have good news. God meets us in the desert. He uses the desolate places of our lives to rebirth our souls, not only with his presence but with a new call to purpose and destiny. I hope you will join me through the pages of this book as we journey through the desert places of our lives to a miraculous encounter with God.

If you're wondering whatever happened to Tracy, know that when I later checked on her, I found she was making progress through her pain. Through God she has both hope and a future. Like you, she's going to be okay.

Trip to the Oasis

At the end of each chapter, we will linger by an oasis where you will read a psalm as your own prayer. Note that our first psalm,

Psalm 43, is by an unknown writer who, like you, is trying to find God in the midst of difficulties. As you read it, say these words to the Lord in the quietness of your heart.

> You are God my stronghold.
>> Why have you rejected me?
> Why must I go about mourning,
>> oppressed by the enemy?
> Send me your light and your faithful care,
>> let them lead me;
> let them bring me to your holy mountain,
>> to the place where you dwell.
> Then will I go to the altar of God,
>> to God, my joy and my delight.
> I will praise you with the lyre,
>> O God, my God.
>> Why, my soul, are you downcast?
>> Why so disturbed within me?
> Put your hope in God,
>> for I will yet praise him,
>> my Savior and my God. (Ps. 43:2–5)

PRAYER EXPERIENCE

Dear Lord,

I have to admit there are times I feel rejected by you. When I look at the desolate place I am in, I'm not sure if I even have the right or power to hope in you. But yet like the psalmist, I am calling to you. I am asking you to appear in my life and to guide me through the desert with your power and truth. I'm asking that you strengthen my heart, soul, and spirit to do your will and to find my purpose. I choose to praise you. For you are my Savior and my God. I put my hope in you. Please guide me through my circumstances by your spirit, power, and truth as I read this book. Anoint me with hope and understanding as well as your grace and goodness as I read. For I need to discover your life-changing love and joy.

In Jesus' name,

Amen

Chapter Video

Go to www.IgniteMyFaith.com or use the QR code at the end of the book to watch the videos that correspond to each chapter. Click on Chapter Videos, then the chapter number. For this chapter, select Chapter 1.

2

Finding God in Your Circumstances

If the answer to every prayer came immediately, how would we ever become acquainted with the Lord Himself?

—Andrew Murray[1]

Something terrible happened today:

- A family went hungry because they couldn't afford groceries.
- A young woman's doctor told her, "It's cancer."
- A family was left to pick up the pieces after a fire charred their home.
- A woman's husband told her he'd never loved her and that he's leaving her for her best friend.
- A family buried a loved one who died too soon.

Believe me, this is an incomplete list of the troubles happening everywhere. Perhaps you too have found yourself swamped with heartaches and difficulties and you're wondering, *Where is God?*

This is such a great question that I would like to invite you to come with me on a quest to search for God. And I happen to have the directions as written in Jeremiah 29:13, which says, "You will seek me and find me when you seek me with all your heart."

So if the way to God is through a seeking heart, we're well on our way to discovering his whereabouts.

I'm going to start our search for God by telling you of my latest adventure through trial.

I Choose Happy

The Christmas season is difficult for me. I'm good up to Christmas day as I'm surrounded by my husband and children. But the day after I sometimes become trapped in traumatic memories as I relive the day that forever changed my life. I remember the moment I put baby Laura in her lavender dress; the moment I buckled her into her car seat; the moment I turned to my mother and said, "Nothing but nothing would keep me from missing the day after Christmas sales."

> So if the way to God is through a seeking heart, we're well on our way to discovering his whereabouts.

Those words still haunt me.

The morning of this past December 26, I told myself it was okay to grieve over my daughter's accident that happened over twenty years ago. As I sunk into the shadows of the past I recalled my mom and me pushing Laura's stroller through the mall; Laura playing peekaboo with the hem of her dress; my mom and me seeing a crew from the local news station patrolling the mall, searching for a story.

Those memories flickered through my mind, but when the anniversary of the hour that so changed our lives approached, I crawled into my bed and pulled up the covers and wept. I remembered driving home in a sprinkling of rain; the red taillights ahead of me; the car screeching out of control; the minivan looming ahead of us; then the collision. I remember struggling to find Laura in the wreckage and running into the freeway, where I found her in her car seat, unresponsive. A man, a former Vietnam medic, ran out of a house across the street to help us. Other people stopped too, including the news team I'd seen in the mall. They filmed the wreckage, glad to have finally found their story for the evening news.

After a day of revisiting the traumatic memories, I realized I'd let myself slide into a dark place. And though I vowed I would spring back the following day, my heartaches continued. A family member called weeping because a loved one had slipped down another rung in his journey into Alzheimer's. One of my best friends called to tell me that her disease had worsened and now, along with realizing that her life dreams would never come to fruition, she was struggling for life itself. And a young friend arrived at my door, weeping because her Marine husband was soon to be deployed.

That night, I decided to cheer myself up with some "happy" movies on the Hallmark channel. But even my happy movies turned out to be tearjerkers.

Though I'd cried myself to sleep that night, God woke me as I was sniffling through my dreams. He spoke clearly: "You can choose to be happy."

I answered, "I know. I teach that in my seminars."

God seemed unimpressed. "What do you choose now?" he asked me.

In a whiny voice I sniffled a reply. "I choose to be happy."

God said, "Abide with me."

The next morning, though my tears still threatened, I thought about my midnight conversation with God. As the day wore on I continued to whisper to myself, "I *do* choose to be happy." Soon I was able to keep my gloomy thoughts in check. All the things I'd grieved over earlier were still sad, but God's presence cheered me as he reminded, "Abide with me."

"Yes, Lord."

His spirit whispered to mine, "You cannot see your trials from my perspective or understand what I am doing."

"I *will* trust you."

"If you abide with me."

Sometime after lunch, I found myself laughing with friends and realized I was no longer fretting over my worries. When the worries came to mind, I'd pray, "Lord, I know you have a plan. I'm choosing happiness as I abide with and trust you."

A strange thing began to happen—the incoming news from my friends and family took a turn for the better. At every piece of good news I rejoiced in the Lord, not because my trials were over but because I could see the hand of God at work.

> "Lord, I know you have a plan. I'm choosing happiness as I abide with and trust you."

It caused me to think of Romans 8:28, which states, "All things God works for the good of those who love him, who have been called according to his purpose." Those words are sometimes hard to take when you are in the midst of a bitter loss. At the time of our heartache, we're not too keen on exchanging that which we've lost for purpose. But if we can take our eyes off our grief for a moment, we *will* find good. As for my example, God gave me good despite my dance with sorrow because

- he guided me as I sought him
- he gave me a glimpse of his great love for me
- he gave me strength to trust him
- he gave me joy despite my circumstances
- he abided with me

Note that whatever God did for me through my sorrow, he will certainly do for you too.

Seeking God

The Bible says in Matthew 7:7–8, "Ask and it will be given to you; seek and you will find; knock and the door will be opened to you. For everyone who asks receives; the one who seeks finds; and to the one who knocks, the door will be opened."

But perhaps, for some of us at least, we need a reason to seek him. I think Andrew Murray summed it up when he said, "There must be a trial. For as long as the flesh has everything agreeable and according to its inclinations, the soul will never wholly and with power cling to the Lord."[2]

> **Many of our trials serve as invitations to cling to God.**

I believe this to be true. Many of our trials serve as invitations to cling to God. Can we learn how to cling to him without such a test? I don't think I could have. Months before the accident that put my daughter into a coma, the Lord strongly impressed upon me that I was about to go through a deep trial. I argued with him, "No, Lord. Teach me what you want me to know without a trial. I'm willing to listen. Really!"

I continued to plead until God convicted me to pray, "Lord, if this trial ahead of me is the only way you can teach me, I'm willing to walk though the fire."

So, though I was shocked that the trial went beyond my worst fears, I can't say it was unanticipated. However, knowing a trial was coming didn't make it any easier. For months after the crash, I was numb with terror and shock. I screamed my prayers in silence: "Lord, wake my daughter from her coma!"

As the days turned into weeks, then into months, it hurt terribly to think that God would neither heal my baby nor release her to heaven. But it was in that time that I sought God harder than I'd ever sought him before. And he showed up. Almost a year after the accident, when I nestled my newborn son into Laura's arms, Laura awoke from her coma. God brought my little girl home.

Perhaps the greatest miracle of all that came from my trial was this: when I clung to God, I didn't have to search for him, for I found I was wrapped in his loving arms.

Despite the Trauma

Though you can't always choose your circumstances, you can choose to be happy. For example, years ago I had a dear friend who was miraculously healed of cancer, but instead of being joyful that the battle was won, my friend continued to live with the trauma of her former illness. She asked me privately, "How could God have even let it happen?"

My friend had a traumatized spirit. But we can rid ourselves of a spirit of trauma if we but ask:

Lord, please free me from the spirit of trauma that has so tormented me. Please replace that spirit of trauma with your spirit of peace. In your name I can say, "Peace be still."

I let go of the hysteria, bad memories, flashbacks, pain, grief, trauma, and loss and give all these things to you as a gift. You are in charge of my broken heart. I trust you to heal it and to soothe my emotions, spirit, and soul with the balm of your love, in the name of Jesus and in the power of his blood and his resurrection power. Amen.

(I would have been smarter if I'd prayed this prayer before I slipped into my day of remembering.)

Still, how do we dispel the myth that happiness comes from our circumstances? In her book *How to Find Selfless Joy in a Me-First World*, Leslie Vernick tells the story of a miserable man who lived an almost perfect life. Leslie explained that Adam was a man who had it all—a good marriage, a great job, beautiful kids, a lovely home, and three cars he drove just for fun. Yet he sat in Leslie's office with tears streaming down his face and said, "I'm still not happy. What's wrong with me?"

Leslie explained his condition this way:

When the Bible speaks of happiness or joy, it is not simply referring to the temporary pleasure that comes from having a great time . . . vacation or enjoying a delicious meal. Joy is not even the inner satisfaction we feel when we do a good job or the pleasure we experience when we gather together as a family for a holiday celebration. Those are all wonderful feelings, but they are fleeting, meant only to be tastes of something that points us towards the greatest pleasure and joy of all—knowing the presence of God.[3]

> Though you can't always choose your circumstances, you can choose to be happy.

And that's the nature of the choice we are making when we choose joy. We are trading our sorrows for the presence of God.

Choosing joy is choosing to abide with God.

Abiding with God

You might be surprised to discover that the best place to find God is within yourself. Not that you *are* God, but God wants to abide in you. In order to abide with God, you first have to make his acquaintance personally. You can do so with a prayer such as:

> Dear Lord,
>
> I believe in you. I believe that your Son came to die on the cross for my sins so that I can walk with you, pure and blameless in your eyes. Please forgive me for my sins, and thank you for lifting them off me and onto Jesus. Jesus, thank you for dying in my place, thank you for rising from the dead so I can know God. Holy Spirit, you are welcome in my life. In the name of Jesus, amen.

This prayer is only the first step to abiding with God. But we know that when we pray such a prayer, God's very presence enters our lives so that our bodies become his temple (1 Cor. 3:16). So if his Holy Spirit is in us, we abide with him whenever we recognize his presence.

Glimpsing His Great Love for Me

It's hard to seek God when you think he's hiding behind indifference. But as we take a closer look we'll discover that's just not the case. God cares about our pain. Even Mary, the sister of Martha, found that to be true when she wept at his feet and admonished, "If you had been here, my brother would not have died."

It's interesting that even though Jesus was about to raise her brother from the dead, he was moved by her grief and wept with her.

Last September, I visited a wonderful church camp. One evening, Jeannie, the mother of a handicapped child, shared a profound dream in which she saw herself as a prisoner behind tightly spaced bars. She tried to reach out to Jesus but couldn't, so she sat down and wept over her disabled daughter. As she wept, she asked the Lord, "Do you even care? Do you feel my pain?"

That's when the hand of the Lord reached through the bars. She grasped it and looked up to see Jesus, her pain reflecting in his eyes. Jeannie said, "That dream helped me to realize he does care. I wasn't alone. He was walking through my heartache with me."

What a wonderful picture. Jesus weeps when we weep. So despite how alone you feel, you are actually surrounded by his great love. For as the apostle Paul said in Ephesians 3:17–19, "And I pray that you, being rooted and established in love, may have power, together with all the Lord's holy people, to grasp how wide and long and high and deep is the love of Christ, and to know this love that surpasses knowledge— that you may be filled to the measure of all the fullness of God."

> Choosing joy is choosing to abide with God.

Finding the Treasures in Difficulties

In her book *I Saw the Lord*, Anne Graham Lotz, daughter of Billy and Ruth Graham, tells the story about the time her mother sent her a birthday present wrapped in plain brown paper. When she opened it, she found a gaudy Mexican basket stuffed with tissue paper. Not realizing that one of the wads of tissue paper contained a treasure, she threw the wads into the trash. It wasn't until she spoke with her mother that she realized her mistake. Digging through her garbage bin, she unwrapped each piece of wadded tissue until she found her present, a small gold ring with a lapis lazuli stone taken from the flooring of the Palace of Shushan. Anne asks, "What priceless treasure are you in danger of throwing out, simply because of the way it was packaged? Could it be the treasure of *seeing Him*? Sometimes God wraps his glory in hard circumstances or ugly obstacles or painful difficulties, and it never just occurs to us that within those life-shaking events is a fresh revelation of Him."

She continues, "Stop resisting Him. Stop resenting Him. Stop complaining. Stop feeling sorry for yourself. Stop demanding what you want. Stop focusing on the outer wrappings of yourself and your circumstances. Adjust your attitude. Change your mind about things—about yourself—about others—about Him. Relax in total trust. He knows what He's doing. Unwrap the package! Let go and look up! Let Him open the eyes of your heart. OPEN YOUR EYES. *Open your eyes* to the vision of His glory! Prayerfully and expectantly, sincerely open your eyes to Him!"[4]

So, the answer to our question—where is God?—is simply this: our God of miracles is right here with us now. We may not see or even recognize his presence, that is, until we're far enough down our path that we can look back. Then our eyes will be opened and we will see he was with us, holding us, loving us, and accomplishing his good in amazing ways, even when we were too close to our circumstances to see that he was at work all along.

Trip to the Oasis

In the prayer of Psalm 3, we find David praying as he was on the run from his enemies. Let's turn his prayer into a prayer of our own.

> LORD, how many are my foes!
>   How many rise up against me!
> Many are saying of me,
>   "God will not deliver him."
> But you, LORD, are a shield around me,
>   my glory, the One who lifts my head high.
> I call out to the LORD,
>   and he answers me from his holy mountain.

I lie down and sleep;
    I wake again, because the LORD sustains me.
I will not fear though tens of
       thousands
    assail me on every side.
Arise, LORD!
    Deliver me, my God!
Strike all my enemies on the jaw;
    break the teeth of the wicked.
From the LORD comes deliverance.
    May your blessing be on your people.

> Jesus weeps when we weep. So despite how alone you feel, you are actually surrounded by his great love.

PRAYER EXPERIENCE

Dear Lord,

I want to trust you with my circumstances, I really do. But my heart is full of fear and grief. I don't understand what you are up too, and there's so much at stake that I must ask for your loving-kindness and mercy. So I fall on my knees and ask for healing, help, guidance, and provision. But at the same time, Lord, know that I praise and worship *you* more than I desire my own way. For I will not raise any false idols against you, not even the idol of the desires of my heart. I ask you to take my problems and turn them into miracles. I declare that I trust you and bow to your will. Rise up like a shield to protect me from my enemies. Give me strength and help me to see you and know you are with me.

In the name of Jesus,
Amen

To pray with me, go to www.IgniteMyFaith.com, click on Chapter Videos, then Chapter 2.

3

Five Keys to Surviving Difficult Times

If you will wait on the Lord, He will become all you need.

—Andrew Murray[1]

A few days after a devastating earthquake in Haiti, a friend said to me, "How could a good God cause so much suffering? I mean, if God is a God of love, then where's the proof?"

Good question. Why would God allow things like the shifting of the earth to cause the collapse of whole cities? Why would he allow people to die in the rubble of their crushed homes? Is God a sadist, set to torture us into repentance? Does it please him to see us in pain?

I told my friend, "I think we forget that we still live on earth, not heaven. Earth is a place where evil and heartache exist, where unspeakable sin, evil, and demons roam, and where natural disasters take lives. One day, true believers will have passed this test called *earth* and will graduate to our heavenly home with God. In that day, both evil and heartache will be a distant memory."

"That's one of the better explanations I've heard," she said, her frown deepening. "But do you think God was punishing the people of Haiti?"

"If he was, we're all in trouble, for when Jesus discussed why a tower had fallen and killed eighteen men back in the days of his earthly ministry, he said this: 'Do you think they were more guilty than all the others living in Jerusalem? I tell you, no! But unless you repent, you too will all perish'" (Luke 13:4–5).

> One day, true believers will have passed this test called *earth* and will graduate to our heavenly home with God. In that day, both evil and heartache will be a distant memory.

Jesus' explanation means we could *all* be in danger. And though this news isn't very comforting, Jesus made a good point. We are all wicked, every one. The apostle Paul even said so in Romans: "For all have sinned and fall short of the glory of God." But the good news is, as Paul continued, "And [we] are justified freely by his grace through the redemption that came by Christ Jesus" (Rom. 3:23–24).

To receive that grace we must ask for it. For when we seek it, we find it. When we repent, we are made right with God.

But does being right with God mean we will be protected from earthquakes and other calamities?

Not necessarily. Just a couple of days ago, I stood at the reception desk at the Denver TV station where I often host the *Denver Celebration* TV show. Trish, my producer, told me, "We're not taping a show this afternoon."

"Why not?" I asked.

"Our guest was to be David Hames from Compassion International. He was in the Montana Hotel when the quake hit two weeks ago."

"Is he okay?"

She shook her head and lowered her voice to a whisper. "He's still there. In the rubble. He was such a godly man with two little kids and a wife. It's so sad."

My heart sank. It's hard to imagine why God would allow something like this to happen to this wonderful man while he was on a mission of mercy. What terrible suffering for David, his family, and his colleagues at Compassion International, a great ministry that helps feed and educate children.

> "Though he slay me, yet will I hope in him" (Job 13:15).

Even if you held a gun to my head, I couldn't explain why this happened to David or any other victim of the quake. Though I can tell you that God loves the injured and the missing, as well as the departed. I know that God loves David and his family and those who worked beside him in ministry. But the question is this: did God *author* the quake? Maybe. Or maybe it, like so many of our troubles, was an event influenced by the enemy. In the book of Job, we get a glimpse of Satan standing before God, pleading his case against a godly man. Satan demanded that God test Job to see if his difficulties would cause him to curse God (Job 1:11).

God agreed and allowed Job to be tested in a series of troubles in which Job lost his children, his flocks, and finally his health. Job did not curse God but said instead, "Though he slay me, yet will I hope in him" (Job 13:15).

Job not only passed the test demanded by Satan, but by the end of Job's life, he had received restoration and blessings from God, even more than before.

So now that we've touched on a few of the reasons why bad things happen, I want to show you a more comprehensive list. Bad things happen:

- randomly (we live in a fallen world system)
- because of sin (sin and evil are alive)
- because of choices (made by ourselves or others)
- through natural disasters and accidents (we're approaching the time of sorrows; see Matthew 24:4–14)
- because of the enemy (he wants to torment us and to see us fail before God)
- for testing (to prove us to our enemy, Satan)
- for repentance (to draw our souls out of harm's way)
- for judgment (God will not be mocked, and though God is a God of love, he is also a God to be feared; fear of God is the beginning of wisdom)
- for God's glory (to prove God can turn difficulties into miracles)

In the case of the earthquake in Haiti, I can only speculate as to which of these reasons was *the* reason the island of Haiti shook. God never told Job the *why* of his troubles, and neither does God tell us. Even so, I can tell you that we can trust God through both pain and suffering. As we trust him, an amazing thing happens. We discover that despite our circumstances, God is a holy, loving God who can turn tragedy into miracles. And speaking of miracles, God wants us to respond to tragedy by becoming his hands and feet to care for and help those in need. So maybe the question we should ask ourselves is why do *we* allow suffering?

When we show love to others, God's presence is with us.

We can't come to the rescue of all, but there's plenty of suffering we *can* do something about. When we get the opportunity, do we respond or ignore the need because of our apathy or busyness? How much suffering would be alleviated if we would rise to action?

John Wesley, a seventeenth-century English preacher, once said, "Do all the good you can, in all the ways you can, to all the souls you can, in every place you can, at all the times you can, with all the zeal you can, as long as ever you can."[2]

When we show love to others, God's presence is with us.

Ways to Overcome

Perhaps we can't always know the why of disasters and calamities. But even when God doesn't reveal the reason, he always reveals himself. To see God and to find the strength to endure, we need to be sure we are:

- creating a pure heart (rooting out that which hinders God)
- praising God in our circumstances
- understanding who we are
- walking by faith
- focusing on God

Creating a Pure Heart

There are times we must suffer for choices we've made. Whether God is disciplining us or not, it always helps our situation if we turn our hearts to God and stand forgiven.

One evening, King David couldn't sleep, so he stood on the roof of his palace overlooking the temple. There he could see the women as they came in for their monthly purification-ritual bath. That's when he saw her, the lovely Bathsheba, Uriah's wife. Dazzled by her beauty, he summoned her to the palace. It was there, in the king's own bed, that Bathsheba became pregnant with David's child.

Now David had a real problem. To hide his deed, he called for Uriah to come home from battle so that he would sleep with Bathsheba. But Uriah, David's faithful soldier and friend, slept on the palace step instead of with his wife. Now David had a bigger problem. He solved it by sending Uriah back to battle with a note to the commander with instructions to put Uriah in the thick of battle, then to pull out, leaving this man behind to be slaughtered by the enemy.

His plan worked perfectly, and when David thought he'd gotten away with murder, the prophet Nathan arrived in his throne room with news that God would judge David because of his wicked deed.

David repented and renewed his heart before God. He prayed these magnificent words found in Psalm 51:

> Create in me a new, clean heart, O God, filled with clean thoughts and right desires. Don't toss me aside, banished forever from your presence. Don't take your Holy Spirit from me. Restore to me again the joy of your salvation, and make me willing to obey you. Then I will teach your ways to other sinners, and they—guilty like me—will repent and return to you. (vv. 10–13 TLB)

Perhaps, unlike David, you might be feeling pretty good about yourself because you've never done anything as bad as David did. But even so, you may have a few things that are keeping you from becoming all you could be. In his book *The Vision and Beyond*, originally published in 1973, David Wilkerson writes about the Christians of the future (who are now the Christians of today).

> Look at the last day Christian, the television addict!
> Look at him—hours and hours for soap operas, comedies, sports—but no time to get alone with God. He turns God off with a dial. He hunts, fishes, travels; plays golf, tennis, and basketball. He goes to movies and parties, and has become a gadabout, but he

has no time to read his Bible or pray. Is this the last day Christian who is supposed to walk by faith? Is this the one whose faith will overcome the world? Is this the one who is to prepare for a coming day of persecution and world chaos? Are these the playboy Christians upon whom the ends of the world will fall?

The greatest sin of the future against God is not abusing the body, indulging the flesh, or even cursing His name. The greatest sin against God is simply to ignore Him in a day and age when He is calling so clearly.[3]

How convicting—which leads us to immediately pray, Oh Lord, create in me a clean heart and renew a right spirit within me.

Praising God in Our Circumstances

Tonight I had a difficult phone call. My twenty-two-year-old, newlywed assistant called to tell me her cancer had spread. She'd discovered the disease only a few days before. Renee sounded afraid, but I could hear hope in her voice as she began to tell me all the ways God had moved on her behalf. Instead of letting fear and bitterness take over her thinking, which would have been far too easy, she focused on God's grace. She said things like, "It was good the Red Cross flew my Marine husband back from Hawaii so he could be with me when I got this news" and "It's good that my mom's a nurse, I know she'll take good care of me" and "It's good that so many people are praying for me."

> Perhaps we can't always know the why of disasters and calamities. But even when God doesn't reveal the reason, he always reveals himself.

I'm so proud that Renee can see God's goodness in this moment. Sure, in the coming weeks and months as she faces chemo, she's going to have times of doubt and fear, but as she acknowledges God and his goodness, she will continue to see miracles.

The same goes for you. As you acknowledge God's goodness, you too will see miracles in your own circumstances. As you praise him, you will see his love for you, and in turn, his love will comfort you. So, don't turn your face to the wall and give up. Don't stay in a huff over what God has allowed in your life. As an act of your will, thank God for anything you can, and victory will soon surprise you.

On the day that David was saved from him enemies, he praised God by singing this song (also found in Psalm 18): "I will call upon the LORD, who is worthy to be praised; So shall I be saved from my enemies" (2 Sam. 22:4 NKJV).

Yes, the Lord is worthy to be praised, even when we don't yet have the victory we long for. The more we praise him, the more his presence will strengthen us, and the more joy we will experience despite our troubles. Joy *is* a choice.

Can I hear another, "Praise the Lord"?

Understanding Who We Are

Once, while flying across the country, I had a seatmate who was a famous actor. I'd noticed, back in the terminal, how his celebrity attracted a crowd. I asked him, "What's the weirdest thing people say to you?"

In his deep Mississippi drawl, he said, "It happened to me again the other day. I met this fellow and a couple of days later, I ran into him again. This fellow said, 'I saw you in a movie last night and I turned to my friends and family and said, "There's Gary Grubbs, he's my friend."'"

Gary said, "That man doesn't know me. He doesn't know anything about me. He doesn't know my wife or even if I have children. He doesn't know what I like to do or even what I like to talk about."

Gary was right. The man only knew Gary's celebrity. When it comes to God, I think we have to be careful we don't fall into this trap. Sure, we all know who God is; he's famous, after all. But until we come to faith in God through Christ and through forgiveness of sin, our knowledge of who he is is only head knowledge, not a real heart-to-heart relationship.

But once we have that heart relationship with God, we must not listen to the enemy's whoppers such as "God doesn't care about you. If he did he would never let these terrible things happen. Your present situation is nothing but proof that you're out of favor, forgotten, unloved, despised, and unforgiven."

> The more we praise him, the more his presence will strengthen us, and the more joy we will experience despite our troubles. Joy **is** a choice.

Nothing could be further from the truth. The truth is that the enemy would love to hold you hostage in the area of your identity. He would love for you to believe you are nothing but a lowly orphan in God's eyes. But don't forget, there are no orphans in God's kingdom. You are his child. So much so that he sent his only Son to rescue you from the kingdom of darkness.

Don't let the enemy use your circumstances or past to beat you up concerning who you are in Christ. Romans 8:1 says, "Therefore, there is now no condemnation for those who are in Christ Jesus."

So God doesn't condemn you? Not if you are in Christ Jesus. Like King David, even though your sin may be significant, you are loved, and when you turn your heart to him, you are also forgiven. That means Christ is your friend, your savior, your brother, and your Lord.

Walking by Faith

Our reality with God should not be based on how we feel. For example, someone might say, "This morning, I felt loved by the Lord, but by this afternoon, I felt like he despised me."

Your feelings can change with your mood. Your feelings can lie. Feelings are not true indicators of reality. In fact, feelings are often influenced by the evil one and his mind games. He's the master of warping reality and relaying false reports. Better walk steady in the Lord, knowing that you can trust him to lead you, despite how you feel.

A false report? We get them all the time. For example, the other day I found my son's cat dead under the couch. With my heart pounding, I rushed down the stairs to my husband, exclaiming, "I killed the cat!"

Paul and I went to see the body. And there it was, hidden beneath the back of the recliner sofa, with only its rump showing. We called to the cat. Nothing. We leaned over the couch and poked the cat with a long handled duster. Nothing. I dropped the duster, and the handle clanged against the metal heating duct. The cat did not move. Paul looked at me. "Did you sit on this couch?" he asked.

> Better walk steady in the Lord, knowing that you can trust him to lead you, despite how you feel.

I nodded, and he said, "Then you must have crushed the cat."

Paul tipped the couch so we could remove the body. That's when the cat leapt to its feet. Our perception had been wrong all along. Apparently the cat was under the false assumption that if he couldn't see us, we couldn't see him, or perhaps he thought we'd just go away and leave him alone. Whichever the case, that cat was never dead, he was just ignoring us.

So when it comes to our lives and our perception of God and our circumstances, how do we keep it all straight? The answer is simple: to get God's perspective we must read his Word and pray for truth and guidance. We must, in the name of Jesus, tell the enemy to hush! (Hush, evil one, in the name of Jesus!) Soon you'll start to see things more clearly. But no matter how things seem, you can rely on the knowledge that God *is* guiding you—but to where?

To himself.

Focusing on God

Are you seeking to change your circumstances more than you are seeking God? That's not a good idea, because one of the keys to surviving difficult times is to focus on him, not our troubles. As it turns out, the ability to focus on God holds the secret to experiencing God's love, peace, and victory. Before I describe how to use that key, let's stop for a little bat practice.

It was a crisp October evening in the Pocono Mountains of Pennsylvania. As darkness fell across the campground, the women and I gathered in the pine-raftered lodge to worship.

So, when the all-women-band began to sing praise songs, the crowd responded by lifting their voices as one. As the music swelled, the women closed their eyes and lifted their faces and sang.

The band was magnificent, and the singers had more than talent, they had a heart for God. This was the perfect environment for worship, at least one would think.

After a couple of awe-inspiring songs, one of the women approached the microphone. In a hushed tone of reverence, she said, "God is here. The Lord's presence is with us like never before. He's going to do something new. Keep your eyes focused on him."

As this woman stepped away from the microphone, the worshipers resounded with joy. I closed my eyes, my intent to focus on God. And I did—that is, until I felt a new presence. Something was in the room with us. I peeked out of one eye. *Yes! Something is hovering above the band. Is it a dove?*

I squinted until I realized, *No, no, that would be a bat.*

I noted that the women in the band didn't seem to mind that a bat hovered over them. Their eyes were closed, and those without instruments raised their hands in total worship.

God made bats, I reasoned. *Bats are part of his creation. So there's a bat. So what? We can worship God with a bat.*

I closed my eyes and continued to worship. But then I felt my heart skip a beat. *Something else is happening near me.*

I squinted my eye open again to see the bat was now dive-bombing me and the entire front row.

I was impressed by the lady next to me. Though she too saw the bat, she kept right on worshiping. With her hands raised in praise, she stood in a crouched position, her elbows flapping as she dodged the bat every time it swooped at her head.

> Are you seeking to change your circumstances more than you are seeking God? That's not a good idea, because one of the keys to surviving difficult times is to focus on him, not our troubles.

This was something new—she was still worshiping though under attack from a bat! "Keep standing," I whispered, "it's not going to hurt you."

She nodded and stood a little straighter, still praising God, but with her eyes on the bat.

I closed my eyes again and tried to focus on God. And I really tried. But now I felt a shiver, so I peeked again. Though the praise band was still enraptured in worship, the bat had expanded his territory and was now dive-bombing the entire room of worshipers.

The women crouched, they dodged, but, to my amazement, they kept on singing. *Incredible. God certainly is doing something new.*

I closed my eyes again and really, really tried to focus on God. And I did, until a most disturbing tingle fingered down my spine. I turned again, this time to see two women with raised brooms, each standing across the room from each other, playing what appeared to be a game of badminton with the bat.

Whack. One would knock the bat over the heads of the worshipers to the other player. *Whop*.

Wow, I thought, *that must be what spiritual warfare looks like. How unusual to actually see it.* I turned around and tried to worship again. This time, I really, really, really tried to focus on God, but now, but now . . . the hair on the back of my neck bristled. I turned to see that one of the women had slapped the bat against the far wall of the room with her broom and was sweeping the bat down. I could see her bare hand reaching to grab the bat.

Before I knew it, I was running down the aisle, shouting, "No! No! Don't touch that bat! It could have rabies!"

Too late, she'd already grabbed the bat and threw it into the night where it fluttered away.

I stood behind her in shock. "Did it bite you?" I asked her in a whisper.

She turned around, looking stunned. Though she shook her head no, I wasn't sure I believed her. As I walked back to my seat, I determined to follow up with her after the service. The worship song was ending and the lady who'd instructed us to focus on God was heading back to the microphone.

As I took my seat, she gave me and the women a look of disgust. Her pointed finger swept the room.

"Shame on you. You didn't focus on God," she scolded.

I felt my face burn. *Wait a minute*, I wanted to argue, *these women were under attack. They could have scattered, they could have screamed, but they kept right on worshiping.*

My self-righteous response, though not spoken aloud, was suddenly pierced when one of the members of the band looked surprised. She said, "Did something happen while we were worshiping?"

That's when it hit me. Though the band endured the same attack as the rest of us, they were so focused on worshiping God they hadn't even noticed the attack.

> The more you focus on your circumstances, the greater the chance your circumstances can and will harm you.

Here's what I learned from this experience: just because you walk with God doesn't mean circumstances will never drive you batty. But the key is to focus more deeply on God. However, if you're not careful, you may discover, like my friend who had indeed been bitten by that bat and had to complete a series of rabies shots, the more you focus on your circumstances, the greater the chance your circumstances can and will harm you.

I have good news for you. God is with you in your current crisis. And as you walk arm-in-arm with the Lord, you're going to find a few blessings along the way. Think of it this way—as Andrew Murray once said, "If the answer to every prayer came immediately, how would we ever become acquainted with the Lord Himself? The gifts of the Lord would occupy our attention so much that we would overlook the Lord Himself."[4]

Watch my overview of these five keys to surviving difficult times at www.IgniteMyFaith.com. Click on Chapter Videos, then Chapter 3.

Trip to the Oasis

Pray the Psalm that David prayed when he faced his sin:

> O loving and kind God, have mercy. Have pity upon me and take away the awful stain of my transgressions. Oh, wash me, cleanse me from this guilt. Let me be pure again. For I admit my shameful deed—it haunts me day and night. It is against you and you alone I

sinned, and did this terrible thing. You saw it all, and your sentence against me is just. But I was born a sinner, yes, from the moment my mother conceived me. You deserve honesty from the heart; yes, utter sincerity and truthfulness. Oh, give me this wisdom.

Sprinkle me with the cleansing blood and I shall be clean again. Wash me and I shall be whiter than snow. And after you have punished me, give me back my joy again. Don't keep looking at my sins—erase them from your sight. Create in me a new, clean heart, O God, filled with clean thoughts and right desires. Don't toss me aside, banished forever from your presence. Don't take your Holy Spirit from me. Restore to me again the joy of your salvation, and make me willing to obey you. Then I will teach your ways to other sinners, and they—guilty like me—will repent and return to you. (Ps. 51:1–14 TLB)

PRAYER EXPERIENCE

Dear Lord,

Thank you for hearing my prayer for a renewed, clean heart. Thank you that you are answering that prayer.

Now I look to you as I lay down my circumstances at your feet. I ask that you open my eyes to see you as you guide me through. I praise you that you are going to use this circumstance in a way that will bring us closer together. I praise you that I can trust you, I praise you for your love for me. And I worship you and say, I love you!

Thank you for letting me be your child. Help me to walk with you, by faith, not looking at my troubles, but by keeping my eyes focused on you.

In Jesus' name,

Amen

4

Giving Your Troubles to God

The Christian life is not a constant high. I have my moments of deep discouragement. I have to go to God in prayer with tears in my eyes, and say, "O God, forgive me," or "Help me."

—Billy Graham[1]

A couple of years ago, I was speaking at a women's event in Nebraska. I shared a story about a suicidal woman from Iowa who knelt on the carpet and gave God her burdens. I related the woman's joy as she ran to tell her daughter, "I'm free, I'm free."

After the event, a young woman named Darla rushed to my side. "Linda, Trina, one of our women, just got an unbelievable phone call!"

"What happened?"

"Trina's mother, Betsy, called to say that she'd given up on life. She'd planned to end her life after tonight's event. She'd only attended so she could tell her daughter good-bye."

"Oh my!"

Darla tried to catch her breath. "But Betsy was so struck by the story of the Iowa woman who gave her burdens to God that she decided to leave early, go home, and kneel before the Lord. When she got to her bedroom, she knelt on the carpet and gave God her burdens. She just called her daughter to say, 'I'm just like the women Linda told us about, God set me free!'"

What a thrill to hear how God changed Betsy's life. You can see more of this story on www.IgniteMyFaith.com under Chapter Videos, Chapter 4.

Can God change your life? Absolutely. It's just a matter of transferring your problems from yourself to God.

Giving It Up

So what's in your hand? Is that worry, burdens, heartache, pain, and fear I see? Why are you lugging that around? What if you knew someone wanted to carry these burdens for you?

There is someone. Jesus himself said, "Come to me, all you who are weary and burdened, and I will give you rest. Take my yoke upon you and learn from me, for I am gentle and humble in heart, and you will find rest for your souls. For my yoke is easy and my burden is light" (Matt. 11:28–30).

The disciple Peter said, "Give all your worries and cares to God, for he cares about you" (1 Pet. 5:7 NLT).

Let me share a true-life allegory to illustrate the point I'm trying to make. When I was working on my novel *A Taste of Fame* with my co-writer, Eva Marie Everson, we decided to go on a field trip to New York City, where part of the novel takes place.

I flew into JFK from Colorado, and Eva flew in from Florida. When we met in the terminal, I said, "Let's grab a taxi to our hotel."

"I have a better idea. Let's start our New York adventure now," Eva said. "I vote we take the subway."

"Are you sure?" I asked, struggling to pull my luggage as we walked. "I mean, I'm not sure I can manage all this baggage."

Eva teased, "So what all do you have there?"

I stopped to demonstrate. "Well"— I tapped the top of my huge, hardcase suitcase—"I've got this empty suitcase so I can do a little Christmas shopping, and then"—I pointed at my overhead-size travel bag—"here are my clothes"—and I pointed at my rolling business case. "I've got my computer and office here, and of course"—I adjusted the strap of my purse on my shoulder—"I've lugged my purse along. It alone weighs in at about twenty-five pounds."

> Can God change your life? Absolutely. It's just a matter of transferring your problems from yourself to God.

"That's a lot of stuff," Eva said as she demonstrated the ease of pulling her one large suitcase with a single finger. "But I think you can make it. Besides, how are we going to write about New York if we don't experience it?"

I agreed, and the next thing I knew we were on the subway and heading into the belly of New York City. Everything went pretty well until the subway came to a halt. "End of the line," a voice garbled from the overhead speaker.

Eva and I exchanged glances before we followed the crowd out the subway door and onto the platform. That's when I saw the stairs.

"So where's the elevator?" I asked a nearby policeman. He simply turned his back and looked the other way.

"I don't think there *is* an elevator," Eva said as she lugged her case to the bottom rung of the narrow metal staircase. I watched as she easily bumped her case up the stairs. Determined to follow,

I draped my heavy purse around my neck, balanced my computer case on top of my small suitcase and held them together by their handles with one hand. Then with my other hand I lifted my large hardback case onto the narrow step in front of me. I slowly began to bump up the stairs, dragging one set of suitcases while I lifted and balanced the other—one step after the other with a bump, grunt, pull. But my problem was that the steps were narrower than my feet, not to mention my baggage.

> I'm wondering if, figuratively speaking, you're struggling with your baggage. If so, I can imagine Jesus standing beside you, asking, "May I take that?"

About halfway up, I began to sway between my luggage. This was it! I was about to fall and there was nothing I could do.

Eva called down from the top of the stairs. "I wish I could help you, but I can't leave my suitcase."

Just then, a teen bounded up the stairs next to me. He stopped. "Can I take your bag?" he asked.

Take my bag? As in steal it? I could feel my brows arch into my hairline. I'd heard this could happen.

But as I swayed there before him, moments from breaking my neck, I gulped and handed over my large case. "You can have it," I said, meaning it.

I was amazed when the young man ran up the stairs, then waited for me at the top. "Here you go," he cheerily said before running off to join his friends.

Eva and I stared after him. "That was a miracle," we agreed.

This miracle happened three more times before we reached our final stop. Each time I got stuck on a staircase, a young man stopped to help.

How grateful I was. I couldn't have made it through the subway if there had been no one to carry my burdens.

I'm thinking the same thing might be true of you. I'm wondering if, figuratively speaking, you're struggling with your baggage. If so, I can imagine Jesus standing beside you, asking, "May I take that?"

What are you going to say to him? You have a choice; are you afraid he's going to steal your so-called "control" or are you ready to be free?

Perhaps it's time to trust the Lord. If you're ready to hand over your burdens, pray this along with me:

Dear Lord,

I'm ready to let go. I'm ready to give up control of my burdens. From now on, these burdens of _____ are yours. I give them to you to carry. While we're at it, would you worry about them for me? I give you permission to come up with your own solutions. These burdens no longer belong to me, they belong to you. For you say in your Word, "Call on me in the day of trouble; I will deliver you, and you will honor me" (Ps. 50:15).

I'm calling on you now.

In the name of Jesus and by the power of his name and resurrection power, I pray,

Amen

How Long?

Mika told me about the persecution she's faced as one of the few Christians in her community. Besides the persecution, she'd also encountered great sorrow in her personal life, especially regarding her kids. She said, "I've even had people say to me, 'Why would I want to be a Christian? I've seen all the terrible things that have happened to you, and God supposedly loves you? When I compare your life with mine, it makes me want to keep my distance from God.'

"It's been hard," Mika admits. "It seems that the people who don't give a flip about God live a charmed life. They don't lose people they love, have the kinds of tragedies that I've experienced, or have trouble with their kids. Everything in their lives seems perfect. It's not fair! I've felt angry that God would allow the wicked to prosper, while I, his own child, am left to deal with one problem after the other."

You might understand how Mika feels. So did David. We know because he wrote over a dozen "how long" prayers, which are recorded in the Psalms. For example, in Psalm 13 he wrote,

> How long, LORD? Will you forget me forever?
> How long will you hide your face from me?
> How long must I wrestle with my thoughts
> and day after day have sorrow in my heart?
> How long will my enemy triumph over me?
> Look on me and answer, LORD my God.
> Give light to my eyes, or I will sleep in death,
> And my enemy will say, "I have overcome him,"
> and my foes will rejoice when I fall. (vv. 1–4)

Maybe you've even wondered if it's worth following God if only the wicked reap blessings.

Perhaps it's time to do a little comparison between living with God and living without him. Sure, those who refuse him may seem to have it all. But on the other hand, those of us who welcome him into our lives have even greater treasure. We have a God who not only sticks with us in trouble but gives us great blessings in our relationship with him. For example, according to David, God's blessings include the fact that God is:

- listening (Psalm 4)
- providing safety (Psalm 4)

- our joy (Psalm 4)
- merciful (Psalm 6)
- accepting of our prayers (Psalm 6)
- unfailing in his love (Psalm 13)
- our salvation (Psalm 13)
- good (Psalm 13)
- a mighty rock (Psalm 62)
- our refuge (Psalm 62)
- strong (Psalm 62)
- loving (Psalm 62)
- our king (Psalm 74)

The difficulties of our lives pale in comparison to the riches we receive as we draw closer to God. And as for evil men, David writes in Psalm 37, "Do not fret because of those who are evil or be envious of those who do wrong; for like the grass they will soon wither, like green plants they will soon die away. Trust in the LORD and do good; dwell in the land and enjoy safe pasture. Take delight in the LORD, and he will give you the desires of your heart" (vv. 1–4).

> The difficulties of our lives pale to the riches we receive as we draw closer to God.

Yes, the "wicked" may enjoy prosperity for a season, but one day their lives will all come to a tragic end. In this vein, David also said, "For you are not a God who is pleased with wickedness; with you, evil people are not welcome. The arrogant cannot stand in your presence. You hate all who do wrong; you destroy those who tell lies. The bloodthirsty and deceitful you, LORD, detest" (Ps. 5:4–6).

I think that instead of being jealous of those who don't know God, we should pray that their eyes would be opened and that they too would find his forgiveness.

For in the end, not only do we get God, we get his salvation and goodness. Psalm 13 concludes with, "But I trust in your unfailing love; my heart rejoices in your salvation. I will sing the LORD's praise, for he has been good to me" (vv. 5–6).

Dr. J. Vernon McGee, best known for his *Thru the Bible* radio programs, once said,

> We need to recognize that God moves in our lives as believers. We get occupied with men and things and circumstances, and we look at them in reference to our lives instead of walking with God. We do not live above our circumstances but under them . . . When we let circumstances come between us and God, God is shut out, and as a result of that we lose the sense of His presence. We get to the place where there is worry and distress instead of peace in our souls, and we do not feel His fatherly hand upon us . . . We do not see the hand of God in all our circumstances.[2]

> Sometimes we forget we're on an adventure with the Lord and that his presence is with us.

Since we don't want circumstances to get in the way of feeling God's presence, let's pray this:

Dear Lord,

Help me not to get preoccupied with the ease of others. Forgive me for my envy. I lay this sin down at your feet. I ask you to fully restore my sense of your presence.

Open the eyes of those who don't know you so that they can see you. And when it comes to my own circumstances, I take my eyes off comparing myself with others and instead turn my eyes to you.

In Jesus' name,
Amen

Going with God

Moses knew he had stepped into trouble when he led the Israelites out of Egypt and crossed the Red Sea. Not only had these people driven him crazy with their complaints about the menu, they had betrayed God by worshiping a golden calf they'd made from their gold trinkets. Moses was so angry with them that he broke all Ten Commandments at once by throwing the stone tablet against the rocks. He told the Lord he was done leading these people unless God sent someone to go with him.

> Moses said to the LORD, "You have been telling me, 'Lead these people,' but you have not let me know whom you will send with me. You have said, 'I know you by name and you have found favor with me.' If you are pleased with me, teach me your ways so I may know you and continue to find favor with you. Remember that this nation is your people."
>
> The LORD replied, "My Presence will go with you, and I will give you rest."
>
> Then Moses said to him, "If your Presence does not go with us, do not send us up from here. How will anyone know that you are pleased with me and with your people unless you go with us? What else will distinguish me and your people from all the other people on the face of the earth?"
>
> And the LORD said to Moses, "I will do the very thing you have asked, because I am pleased with you and I know you by name." (Exod. 33:12–17)

Sometimes we forget we're on an adventure with the Lord and that his presence is with us.

Let's pray this:

Dear Lord,

I'm so glad that you know me by name. You know my situation and you see the journey before me. I don't want to go unless you go with me. So Lord, I'm extending an invitation to you. Join me, Lord. Be my traveling companion and may your presence guide me as I rest in you.

In the name of Jesus,
Amen

Finding His Rest

Once we figure out that we can trust God with our problems, we can relax in him.

Imagine this: Noah was a man who was given an enormous task by God. Phase one of his project was to build a great boat, an ark, actually. This ark was to be about 448 feet long and 3 stories tall. It had enough volume to pack in 5 1/2 miles of boxcars. So this was no small project to accomplish without power tools. But with such a huge task ahead of him, don't you think it strange that Noah's name means *rest*? Check it out: according to Strong's Greek and Hebrew Dictionary, Noah or Noach means *rest*.[3]

> His message is this—it's time to stop striving, it's time to seek God, cast our burdens on him, follow his lead, and rest in him when it comes to the results.

But here's the thing about Noah—he didn't worry about the design of the ark or sweat the details, he just followed God's instructions. His job was to rest in God and do as God instructed. What would happen if we lived that way?

Let's go back and look at what God said to Moses in the previous section. "The LORD replied, 'My Presence will go with you, and I will give you rest'" (Exod. 33:14).

There it is again—*rest*. Wait a minute, didn't we start this chapter with Matthew 11:28, in which Jesus said he would give the weary *rest*?

I think God is trying to tell us something. His message is this—it's time to stop striving, it's time to seek God, cast our burdens on him, follow his lead, and rest in him when it comes to the results. After all, the results are God's job, not ours, especially when we commit the results to him.

Let's pray this:

Dear Lord,

Thank you that you want me to rest in you. Thank you that I no longer have to strive to figure out my problems, as they now belong to you. I thank you for giving me wisdom and direction as I wait on you. Help me to be faithful in obeying you. Keep me from cheating myself out of resting in you by reclaiming control of my journey. I dedicate both my journey and the final results to you.

In the name of Jesus,
Amen

What a wonderful time we've had with the Lord in prayer, inviting him into our circumstances and letting go of our burdens to discover his rest. What Jesus told the woman who found healing when she touched the hem of his garment is a message he wants you to hear: "Your faith has saved you; go in peace" (Luke 7:50).

Trip to the Oasis

David learned to rest in the Lord though his troubles were many. For example, an ungodly king chased him through hill and valley to take his life, his own son rose up against him, and nations met him in war, yet he was able to pray under the anointing of God's rest. Pray David's prayer yourself:

> The LORD is my light and my salvation—
> whom shall I fear?

The LORD is the stronghold of my life—
    of whom shall I be afraid?
    When the wicked advance against me
    to devour me,
it is my enemies and my foes
    who will stumble and fall.
Though an army besiege me,
    my heart will not fear;
though war break out against me,
    even then I will be confident.
    One thing I ask from the LORD
    this only do I seek:
that I may dwell in the house of the LORD
    all the days of my life,
to gaze on the beauty of the LORD
    and to seek him in his temple.
For in the day of trouble
    he will keep me safe in his dwelling;
he will hide me in the shelter of his sacred tent
    and set me high upon a rock.
    Then my head will be exalted
    above the enemies who surround me;
at his sacred tent I will sacrifice with shouts of joy;
        I will sing and make music to the LORD.
    Hear my voice when I call, LORD;
    be merciful to me and answer me.
My heart says of you, "Seek his face!"
    Your face, LORD, I will seek.
Do not hide your face from me,
    do not turn your servant away in anger;
    you have been my helper.
Do not reject me or forsake me,
    God my Savior.

Though my father and mother forsake me,
    the LORD will receive me.
Teach me your way, LORD;
    lead me in a straight path
    because of my oppressors.
Do not turn me over to the desire of my foes,
    for false witnesses rise up against me,
    spouting malicious accusations.
I remain confident of this:
    I will see the goodness of the LORD
    in the land of the living.
Wait for the LORD;
    be strong and take heart
    and wait for the LORD. (Ps. 27:1–14)

PRAYER EXPERIENCE

Dear Lord,

You've heard my prayers, removed my burdens, and given me your rest. Teach me to abide in you and show me how to come against the enemy when he tries to steal your presence and peace from my heart. Teach me how to rest in you.

In Jesus' name,

Amen

5

Standing Against the Darkness

Before you go into warfare, recognize that it is not you that the devil is afraid of; it is Christ in you!

—Francis Frangipane[1]

I went to hear a famous evangelist in a stadium in Phoenix along with twenty thousand others. I was seated in the balcony, a football field away from the speaker. As I listened to his anointed message, something strange caught my eye. About three rows down from me, I saw a teen make a frightening transformation. His eyes bulged, his tongue stuck straight from his mouth while its tip flicked up then down. Then he began to levitate a foot or two above his chair. The people around him were alarmed. They held on to his arms to prevent him from floating off the balcony. At first I sat stunned, then I joined in the cluster of people who began to pray for this young man. Still, I wondered if this "little trick" was somehow staged by the speaker. But the speaker continued his message, never noticing the commotion. After watching (and praying for) this teenager for over an hour, I knew the truth. This young man was possessed by demons.

When the demons finally submitted to our prayers in the name of Jesus, the change in this teen was remarkable. No longer did he float above his chair or make horrific faces. He looked whole, his body relaxed, his eyes peaceful as he sat quietly in his seat.

How did it even happen that this teen had become possessed? I'll speculate that at some point he opened a door to the occult, perhaps through drugs, illicit sex, occultic practices or worship, a demonic computer game, satanic music, or even his own choice.

I'm not the kind of person who believes there are demons hiding behind every bush, but I do believe that Lucifer and his minions are real, as are his efforts to hurt the people God loves.

Lucifer's story is this: once, before time began, Lucifer (another name for Satan) tried to steal God's worship for himself. As a result, Lucifer and his followers, one third of the angels, were cast out of heaven and now make their residence here on earth (Isa. 14:12).

> Our job is not so much to war against Satan as it is to shine God's light in the dark places of our souls so that we can give God our whole heart.

The plot thickens as Lucifer continues to steal God's worship by holding humankind hostage from worshiping or walking with God. That's why Jesus died on the cross and rose again, to defeat Lucifer's power over sin and death so we could be free. It's God's forgiveness, through the work of Christ on the cross, that destroys Satan's legal claim over us. But the way of escape from the dominion of darkness is simply a choice God offers us, a choice either to worship or to reject him. Meanwhile, Satan is still on the prowl, seeking to harm, destroy, or distract whomever he can (John 10:10).

Is Satan able to harass us, the people of God? Yes, in fact we are at war with him as Ephesians 6:12 explains, "For we do not wrestle against flesh and blood, but against principalities, against powers, against the rulers of the darkness of this age, against spiritual hosts of wickedness in the heavenly places" (NKJV). But while Satan can oppress those of us who belong to God, he cannot possess us. Still, he tries to distract us from "abiding" with Jesus. But I have good news: 1 John 4:4 says, "You, dear children, are from God and have overcome them [the spirit of the antichrist], because the one who is in you [Christ] is greater than the one who is in the world [Satan]."

This is great news! Greater is God in us! This means we don't need to be afraid, but we do need to be on guard. Our job is not so much to war against Satan as it is to shine God's light in the dark places of our souls so that we can give God our whole heart. That's the best way to keep the enemy at bay.

Here are some tips to preparing your heart for more of Christ:

- repent
- embrace humility
- grow good fruit
- tear down strongholds
- shut out the enemy
- rejoice

Repent

I know I bring this up a lot, but we need to keep sin in check. Why? It's simple. God wants us to be holy. The holier we become, the more of Christ's presence we possess, and the more our hearts will become a fortress against our enemy. Psalm 59:17 says, "You are my strength, I sing praise to you; you, God, are my fortress, my God on whom I can rely."

Another reason we need to repent is because this act breaks the stronghold the enemy has over our lives and churches. To illustrate what I mean, let me say that I've been in church groups where the enemy has had a heyday planting sends of discord and offense. This kind of disharmony happens when we play religion instead of loving God and others. When we engage in strife, God is a gentleman and steps out of our way. But when we repent, apologize, and forgive, God steps back into our situations, and his presence and anointing is restored in our lives and churches.

If you need to repent from strife or other sins, pray this along with me:

Dear Lord,

Please forgive me for playing religion instead of loving you more. Forgive me for strife and for trying to have my own way. Also, please forgive me for [name anything on your heart or mind].

I want to be restored to you in a right relationship so that you can more deeply abide in my heart. Your abiding presence will help my heart become a fortress against the enemy.

In the name of Jesus,
Amen

I've got good news concerning your prayer: you are forgiven!

On that note, I do have a word of caution about repentance. If you think you have to continually do penance for that which God has already forgiven you, then you're in trouble. Don't let the enemy convince you to pick up the invoice for your past mistakes. You owe nothing. Jesus already paid the bill. Just be sure to say thanks and abide with him.

Embrace Humility

One definition of the word *humble* as dictionary.com puts it is "not proud or arrogant; modest; to be humble although successful."[2]

God loves the humble. Psalms says that God will save the humble (18:27), will guide the humble (25:9), will sustain the humble (147:6), and will crown the humble with salvation (149:4).

Jesus is our role model when it comes to humility (Matt. 11:29). Jesus loves and blesses the meek. He promised they will inherit the earth (5:5).

In contrast, dictionary.com defines the word *proud* to mean "showing a high opinion of one's own dignity, importance, or superiority."[3] Unfortunately the Word gives those who are proud some bad news. Psalms says that God will pay the proud back in full (31:23), the proud will not endure (101:5), and God keeps his distance from the proud (138:6 TLB).

> Don't let the enemy convince you to pick up the invoice for your past mistakes. You owe nothing. Jesus already paid the bill.

The more we become like Jesus, the more humble we will become. The enemy will have little power over us because when he comes to face off with us, he'll see Jesus and flee.

However, here's a caution. Being humble does not mean you see yourself as defeated. Neither does humility have anything to do with being a coward. Consider the story of Queen Esther.

When she was asked to approach the king to stop a plot to destroy her people, she was afraid for her life. If the king failed to extend his scepter to her, she would face death. Though Esther was humble, she was no coward. So instead of saying, "I'm not worthy. Let someone else go before the king instead of me," she decided to take a chance and humbly approached the king herself. In so doing, she saved her people from slaughter.

Don't buy into the lie that you're not good enough to do those things God is calling you to do. Take courage and step into your destiny with the Lord, just do so with humility and through his power.

Dear Lord,

Help me not to think more of myself than I ought. Give me so much love for others that I do not put myself above them but beside them. Help me to serve you and others in love. Help me to do your bidding with courage.

In Jesus' name,
Amen

Grow Good Fruit

Francis Frangipane once said, "It is better to develop godly virtues than to spend the day praying against the devil. Indeed, it is the joy of the Lord that casts out spirits of depression. It is our living faith which destroys spirits of unbelief; it is aggressive love that casts out fear."[4]

Let's take this a bit further by creating a prayer based on Galatians 5:22–23, which says, "But the fruit of the Spirit is love, joy, peace, patience, kindness, goodness, faithfulness, gentleness and self-control."

Dear Lord,

Help me to develop good fruit. May virtues build up my inner person so that your love replaces hate, your joy replaces depression, your peace replaces fear, your kindness replaces wrath, your goodness replaces wrongdoing, your faithfulness replaces unbelief, your gentleness replaces rudeness, and your self-control replaces wrong actions. Guide me so that I will honor you.

In Jesus' name,
Amen

Tear Down Strongholds

Sometimes, without meaning to, we allow the enemy to have strongholds in our lives. A stronghold is a place where the enemy can gain easy access to our thoughts. But the problem is, it's not uncommon to be unaware that strongholds even exist. Frangipane has some wise words to help us identify our strongholds. He says, "Every area in your thinking that glistens with hope in God is an area that is being liberated by Christ. But any system of thinking that does not have hope, which feels hopeless, is a stronghold that must be pulled down."[5]

> Don't buy into the lie that you're not good enough to do those things God is calling you to do. Take courage and step into your destiny with the Lord, just do so with humility and through his power.

Okay, let's try to identify any strongholds in our lives with this little checkup. Do you feel hopeless in your attitudes about your:

- relationships with spouse, family, co-workers, and/or friends?
- moods, temper, and/or disposition?
- housekeeping?
- checkbook, finances, and/or job?
- addictions and/or weight?
- problems and/or needs?
- faith, devotional life, Bible reading, and/or time with the Lord?

These are but a few areas where strongholds of fear, discouragement, and plain old unbelief can creep into our attitudes. So, if you've said yes to any of the above or you've thought of any other strongholds that God has revealed to you, spend some time in the prayer below:

Dear Lord,

Please forgive me for feeling hopeless in the following situations: _____. Please forgive me for hopelessness, fear, discouragement, and unbelief in these areas. I give these situations to you and ask that you infuse them with both your presence and with hope. I know that I can trust you to move not only in these situations but in my attitudes and heart. Close any portals in these or other areas so the enemy cannot speak to me or spread his lies. Help me to recognize and shush his attempts with the powerful name of Jesus. I praise your holy name for hearing and answering this prayer.

In Jesus' name,
Amen

Shut Out the Enemy

A few months ago I was deep in prayer when I had a startling vision. I saw myself covered in blood from head to foot, crouching on a shiny white path in the shape of a cross. As I gazed on this bloody mess I asked, "Lord, what is this?"

"What do you always pray?" his still, small voice asked me.

I was stunned. "Lord, I always pray that you would cover me with the blood of Jesus." I gulped at the ghastly vision. "Do others see *this* when they look at me?"

"This is how the enemy sees you," the Lord said.

"I must look pitiful."

"Oh no! You look terrifying and powerful. Don't forget, the enemy is afraid of the blood of Jesus."

"Are you saying the enemy is terrified of me and I don't even know I have this power over him?"

"Yes."

The Bible speaks to the truth of this revelation in James 4:7, which says, "Submit yourselves, then, to God. Resist the devil, and he will flee from you."

It's true, we can resist the devil. We can also use the power of the name and blood as well as the authority we have in Christ to send the devil running.

> Dear Lord,
>
> I submit to you, please cover me with the blood of Jesus. You know my situation, and I'd like to ask for your presence to be in the middle of it. If I have any sin hindering my prayers, please reveal it and forgive me. Meanwhile, help me resist the devil. I ask this in the name of Jesus and in the power of his blood. And in the power of the name and blood of Jesus, I say, "Enemy, you must flee. I am putting you on notice, the more you hinder God's work in me, the more God is going to hinder you. You may not speak to me as you have in the past. Those portals are closed by the name, authority, and power of Jesus. Leave now, in Jesus' name."
>
> Lord, I now ask that you tear down this stronghold and turn my situation into a miracle.
>
> In Jesus' name,
> Amen

We should never give up on our prayers for those God has placed on our heart.

These kinds of prayers are a lot easier to pray for yourself than for others. That's because when you pray for yourself, you are choosing to do so as an act of your will. But when you pray for others, you may find yourself coming against a wall of *their* will. But this doesn't mean you can't or shouldn't pray for them. We should never give up on our prayers for those God has placed on our heart.

I was once with a small group of women secluded in a mountain retreat. One of the women, Ella, came into our fellowship with an oppressive spirit. By that I mean Ella, who was a believer, was oppressed by the enemy (but not possessed by him). Her oppression manifested with very unusual and childish behavior complete with jealous fits and outlandish demands. I pleaded with Ella to pray with us. "No!" she said as she continued to rage.

It wasn't until Ella finally agreed to pray that she had her breakthrough. When we prayed together, Ella shut the open portal to the enemy's voice (which in her case was fear of rejection). When Ella was back in her right mind, her precious personality returned and she was most embarrassed by her previous behavior. When Ella closed the portal to the enemy's voice, she no longer allowed fear to influence her behavior. God set her free from the enemy's oppression.

The fact that it's harder to pray for those who are possessed or oppressed doesn't mean you shouldn't pray. After all, God *did* answer our prayers for Ella. However, he answered faster when Ella's prayers were added to ours.

Rejoice

Because we are at war with Satan, he will use every opportunity to attack us in areas such as relationships, finances, health, marriages, family, kids. Why does the enemy care about details of your life such as how you're getting along with your boss? Because if he can steal your joy, he can steal your strength, and the Word teaches us that the joy of the Lord is our strength (Neh. 8:10).

As many believers have discovered, one of the best ways to defeat the enemy is to rejoice—rejoice that you know the Lord through Jesus, rejoice that the Lord loves you and hears your prayers. Rejoice that God has taken your matter in hand and is even now coming to your rescue. "Rejoice in the Lord always. I will say it again: Rejoice!" (Phil. 4:4).

We will cover rejoicing in more detail later, but in the meantime, practice keeping a smile on your lips and praise in your heart, and you'll see the enemy flee.

Don't Get Distracted

Now, with all this talk about the devil and his schemes, let me warn you: it's more important to focus on Jesus than it is to focus on the evil one. Whatever you focus on is what you worship. Never focus on the enemy or he will distract and betray you. It's okay to pray against the enemy, but don't allow yourself to be fearful. Keep your focus on Christ.

If we are not careful, the enemy will distract us by tricking us into focusing on everything but God. This reminds me of the time I was walking down Canal Street in New York. A young woman on my left caught my eye as she spread out her arms and skipped sideways next to me. When I turned to look at her, she slipped behind me and stepped to my right. With my attention diverted, she rammed her arm down my unzipped extra-large purse, in an attempt to grab my wallet.

> Whatever you focus on is what you worship. Never focus on the enemy or he will distract and betray you. It's okay to pray against the enemy, but don't allow yourself to be fearful. Keep your focus on Christ.

Happily, I was able to pull my purse away from her before she could grab my pocketbook. But this pickpocket would've never had access to my pocketbook if I had not been distracted while carrying an unzipped purse. This lesson also applies to us and our spiritual lives. We need to keep our focus on Jesus and close down any open portals to the enemy. This way the enemy cannot distract and rob us. That doesn't mean you can't bind him (zip his access) from your situation; you can and you should. But you shouldn't live in fear of him. For after all, Jesus has already defeated him on the cross.

Okay, you know how to pray against the enemy in the name of Jesus as well as how to pray in the power of Christ's blood and authority. Pray this way whenever you need to banish the enemy from your situation, home, family, job, and church. But as you do, keep this in mind. As Francis Frangipane says,

> Indeed it is of the greatest truth that once the devil recognizes the assault against your life has not pulled you from God but toward Him—once he perceives his temptations are actually forcing you to appropriate the virtue of Christ—the enemy will withdraw."[6]

Happily we already know that what the enemy means for evil, God means for good (Gen. 50:20). You belong to God, so no matter what the enemy is able to accomplish in your life, God will turn the tables on him and turn your disaster into a miracle. You're in a win-win situation. You can't lose.

Trip to the Oasis

David sang this Psalm when he was delivered from his enemies. Since God is delivering us from our enemies, let's join in the prayer of David found in Psalm 18.

> I love you, LORD, my strength.
> The LORD is my rock, my fortress and my deliverer;
>   my God is my rock, in whom I take refuge,
>   my shield and the horn of my salvation, my stronghold.

I called to the LORD, who is worthy of praise,
and I have been saved from my enemies.
The cords of death entangled me;
the torrents of destruction overwhelmed me.
He reached down from on high and took hold of me;
he drew me out of deep waters.
He rescued me from my powerful enemy,
from my foes, who were too
strong for me.
They confronted me in the day of my
disaster,
but the LORD was my support.
He brought me out into a spacious
place;
he rescued me because he de-
lighted in me.
As for God, his way is perfect:
The LORD's word is flawless;
he shields all who take refuge in him.
For who is God besides the LORD?
And who is the Rock except our God?
It is God who arms me with strength
and keeps my way secure.
He makes my feet like the feet of a deer;
he causes me to stand on the heights.
He trains my hands for battle;
my arms can bend a bow of bronze.
You make your saving help my shield,
and your right hand sustains me;
your help has made me great.
You provide a broad path for my feet,
so that my ankles do not give way. (vv. 1–4, 16–19, 30–36)

> You belong to God, so no matter what the enemy is able to accomplish in your life, God will turn the tables on him and turn your disaster into a miracle.

PRAYER EXPERIENCE

Dear Lord,

Thank you that you deliver me from my enemies. I ask that you break their strategic assignments off my life through the blood of Jesus as you guide me with truth and your Holy Spirit. Thank you that you love me so much that you want to be the focus of my life. Give me the ability to keep my eyes on you. Fill me with your virtues and help me to continue to tear down the strongholds in my life so that I will more deeply abide in your presence. Fill me full of your humility so that the evil one will flee. May it be that when he looks for me, he finds you instead.

In the name of Jesus and in the power of his blood,

Amen

You can continue to pray with me at www.IgniteMyFaith.com under Chapter Videos, then Chapter 5.

6

Praying Against the Spirit of Strife

You will never forgive anyone more than God has already forgiven you.

—Max Lucado[1]

Don't you wish you could control your life and the people in it—the way you can control a faithful dog?

"Sit! Stay! Speak! Shut up, you!"

Since we can't take the people in our lives to obedience training where they might learn to roll over at our command, how do you suppose we can keep them on a leash?

We can't.

If we spend our energy trying to make others obey us, then we have a controlling spirit that must be submitted to the Lord with a prayer like:

Dear Lord,

    I give you the control I pretend I have and give up my controlling behavior in exchange for trusting you. Give me a hand in letting go.

In Jesus' name,
Amen

It's far better when we operate in a spirit of love. Operating in love is what Jesus himself taught as the most important commandment. "Jesus replied: "'Love the Lord your God with all your heart and with all your soul and with all your mind.' This is the first and greatest commandment. And the second is like it: "Love your neighbor as yourself." All the Law and the Prophets hang on these two commandments'" (Matt. 22:37–40).

> Since we can't take the people in our lives to obedience training where they might learn to roll over at our command, how do you suppose we can keep them on a leash?
>
> We can't.

Paul, in Ephesians, even recommends that we believers submit to one another "out of reverence for Christ" (Eph. 5:21).

I wonder what our homes, families, and churches would look like if we all operated this way? I imagine unselfish love would cure many of our pesky relationship crises. To back this up, I'd like to take a moment to apply this Love Principle to those readers with spouses. If you're single, please keep reading because I think the Love Principle might come in handy in your relationships as well.

Do you feel bored, frustrated, blah, or disgruntled toward your spouse? Maybe it's because somewhere along the way you've lost your ability to connect.

In cases like this, the best solution is to apply the Love Principle. Let me illustrate in the story set in rhyme (my apologies to real poets).

The Love War

"I'm tired of him," she told her friend
    as she sat in her chair.
"I'd like to make him pay
    for never showing that he cares.
What can I do to break his heart?
    When he's so cold to me?
I'd leave him now if only
    it would pain him to be free."
"If you would like to make him pay,"
    her friend said with a grin.
"Then listen close, I know a way
    that breaks the hearts of men.
Before you take him into court
    to break your marriage vows.
You must pretend that you love him,
    and let me tell you how.
Go home and hold your husband close
    and tell him that he's dear.
Let him fall in love with you.
    Erase his every fear.
Then when his heart belongs to you
    this is how you'll win.
March him in before the judge
    so fast his head will spin.
Demand divorce and break his heart
    so he at last may know.
The hurt he caused you through the years
    Will be a stinging blow."
She did as planned with these results,
    which may seem very strange.
She played at love and came to find
    an unexpected change.

It worked so well she had to tell
    her friend which she did call.
"I never knew he is the best
    husband after all.
When he fell for me, I fell for him
    and now you'll never guess,
when we renew our wedding vows
    I'll wear my wedding dress.
I'm packing for a special trip,
    our second honeymoon.
So thank you for your great advice
    that changed my heart and tune."
The lesson here is plain to me
    and I am glad to tell,
that if you want a loving spouse
    you must be one as well.

The Love Principle

As my poem illustrates, love is an attitude. An attitude of love can go a long way in positively affecting all our relationships. Charles Swindoll said,

> The remarkable thing we have is a choice every day regarding the attitude we will embrace for that day. We cannot change our past . . . We cannot change the fact that people will act in a certain way. We cannot change the inevitable. The only thing we can do is play on the one string we have, and that is our attitude."[2]

We should operate in an attitude of love instead of an attitude of pride, that is, unless we want God himself to oppose us. James 4:6 says, "God opposes the proud but shows favor to the humble." And if you've ever seen an episode of *American Idol*, the televised singing competition, you may have noticed the negative effects of a prideful attitude, like when a cocky contestant is shocked when the judges oppose his plans to win a recording contract just because he can't carry a tune.

Romans 12:3 backs up this truth with these words: "For by the grace given me I say to every one of you: Do not think of yourself more highly than you ought, but rather think of yourself with sober judgment, in accordance with the measure of faith God has distributed to each of you."

> I imagine unselfish love would cure many of our pesky relationship crises.

Handling Controlling People

Have you ever had anyone try to correct you? Don't get me wrong, correction can be good for our souls if given in the spirit of love or even guidance. But sometimes correction can be used as a tool of manipulation. The best way to analyze correction you might receive is to ask God to show you the truth of the matter.

Many years ago, my then-publisher fired and replaced their editors. As is often the case in such situations, the new publishing team was quick to abandon projects already in progress in an effort to make room for new projects. I'll never forget the morning I received a phone call from the new brass. Augusta told me, "Linda, I hate to tell you this, but we've evaluated your new manuscript. You are a terrible writer. We think you should never write again."

The words were devastating, and as I later learned, untrue. As I found out a year later, no one at the house had even read my manuscript. The call was a simple dismissal because the new editorial team was unfamiliar with me.

In this time of crisis, Augusta's words shook me to my core. I sought the Lord until he whispered his encouragement to press on. Since that day, my books have ministered to people around the world. Just think, if I had listened to that false criticism, I would have missed God's call on my life.

When you are criticized, listen carefully and apply any truth to your life. But when in doubt as to what the truth is, seek the Lord. He's the one you should submit to. If you are not sure what to do, pray a prayer like this to help you decide:

Dear Lord,
    When I receive criticism, speak to me through it. Show me the truth inside the criticism and how you want me to react. If the criticism is false, help me to see that truth. Guide me in all your ways and let me be kind and humble to those who criticize.

In Jesus' name,
Amen

Another way people may try to control you is through fear. Marcia told me that fear was the tactic her mother-in-law used to control her. Marcia was so afraid of Norma's disapproval that she would do anything to avoid it. But the harder she tried to please Norma, the more disapproval she received.

> The best way to analyze correction you might receive is to ask God to show you the truth of the matter.

Marcia says, "One day I was sitting at a traffic light fuming about my latest encounter with Norma. I wondered, 'What's my problem? How do I let this woman get to me like this?'

"It was like the word *fear* floated across my windshield.

"I instantly went to the Lord and prayed, 'Lord, if Norma is controlling me through fear, I quit the game. From now on, I'm giving my fear of her to you. Replace my fear with peace. In Jesus' name, amen.'"

Marcia says, "I can't explain it, but the next time Norma tried to use this tactic against me, instead of reacting defensively, I laughed. I was stunned by Norma's reaction; she laughed too. Today, since I no longer react to Norma in fear, she's stopped trying to intimidate me. And the funny thing is, I no longer see Norma as the enemy but as a friend. Even Norma seems happier with our relationship."

Could it be that you are allowing fear to creep into your relationships? That's never healthy. Give your fear to God and you'll discover that oftentimes, by changing your reaction, the other person will change their behavior (Prov. 15:1).

Proverbs 29:25 says, "Fear of man will prove to be a snare, but whoever trusts in the LORD is kept safe."

But let me share a word of caution. Though it's not God's plan for us to let fear rule our lives, it's important we follow our instincts. For example, if you feel you shouldn't step into an elevator with a stranger, don't do it. Just step away and wait for the next car. Also, if you find that you are in fear for your own or your children's safety, seek counsel and perhaps protection.

Is It Ever Okay to Stand Back?

The Message says,

> Don't be naive. There are difficult times ahead. As the end approaches, people are going to be self-absorbed, money-hungry, self-promoting, stuck-up, profane, contemptuous of parents, crude, coarse, dog-eat-dog, unbending, slanderers, impulsively wild, savage, cynical, treacherous, ruthless, bloated windbags, addicted to lust, and allergic to God. They'll make a show of religion, but behind the scenes they're animals. Stay clear of these people. (2 Tim. 3:1–5)

It is a dog-eat-dog world out there and not everyone is going to be kind or play fair or even pretend to love God. I'm for turning the other cheek, hanging tough, speaking the truth in love, or even taking a stand when the situation requires it. But there are times it's prudent to step back and stay clear. Think of it this way: if you found yourself alone in a room with a madman with a butcher knife and you had the power to step out and lock the door behind you, would you do it? Of course, you'd run from danger.

You might even call the cops or post a "do not enter" sign on the door in order to spare someone else from being attacked.

Oftentimes, we believers are so afraid of the sin of gossip we don't warn others when warnings are needed. But even the apostle Paul gave his friends warnings, as we can see in 2 Timothy: "Alexander the metalworker did me a great deal of harm. The Lord will repay him for what he has done. You too should be on your guard against him" (4:14–15).

I know of churches that were swindled for millions yet never complained to anyone, including the police. They decided to look the other way so that they would not be embarrassed by their mistake. Their lack of action allowed this same thief access to the offering plates of other churches. If even a simple "Beware!" had been given, many a flock might not have been fleeced. We need to grasp the principle that you can forgive and yet still stop, rebuke, or even send out a warning so that others are not hurt.

Yes, it's wrong to gossip. But no, it's not wrong to warn others of a snake in the grass. "Watch out for that copperhead!"

Please know I am not giving you a license to hurt others with your suspicions or innuendos. Be careful! Do not spread warnings unless you have more to go on than just a funny feeling in your gut. As it turns out, "funny feelings" are often nothing but jealousy or selfish ambition. If you base a warning on your own deceitful desires, you'll harm others out of spite. That's sin. This is why it's so important to pray and practice discernment.

Confronting Someone

We are to make every effort to keep the unity of the Spirit through the bond of peace (Eph. 4:3). However, there are times when it is your responsibility to confront someone in love.

Pastor William had a problem. A young staff member, Jeff, had been busy spreading gossip and lies about him. At first, Pastor William tried to handle this problem by turning the other cheek, allowing the gossip and lies to continue poisoning his congregation.

Finally, when Pastor William saw the great damage Jeff had done, he confronted him for the first time. Jeff wept and apologized, promising he would never gossip and lie about the pastor again, if he could only but keep his job. Pastor William agreed. However, a few days later, Jeff was back to his old tricks, and Pastor William continued his role of Ahab, allowing Jeff's flow of poison to do its damage. Unfortunately, the damage was irreparable.

> Give your fear to God and you'll discover that oftentimes, by changing your reaction, the other person will change their behavior.

The church eventually split, and many precious Christians were hurt in the fallout.

So what could the pastor have done? Perhaps he could have prevented his church from splitting if he had followed Paul's advice, given in Titus 3:10–11: "Warn a divisive person once, and then warn him a second time. After that, have nothing to do with him. You may be sure that such people are warped and sinful; they are self-condemned."

The pastor would have been better off if he or his board had warned Jeff a second time and in a timely manner. If that didn't work, the pastor or the church board should have removed Jeff from both his post and the church. This action would still have caused damage, but the damage would most likely have been less.

I understand that not all of these sorts of situations are as cut and dried as my example. But know this: God has given us power over the enemy. There are times we fight the good fight by turning the other cheek in humility (Matt. 5:39), times we fight by resting in and worshiping God as he fights for us (Josh. 23:9–10), times we fight by speaking the truth in love (Eph. 4:15), and other times we fight by taking a stand (Titus 3:10–11). But the key ingredient in knowing how to fight is prayer.

> Dear Lord,
>
> I'm thinking about a troubling situation and I need help. Please give me wisdom and show me what part you want me to play in this battle. If you want me to be humble, give me your humility. If you want to fight the battle, help me to sit back and rest in you with praise on my lips. If you want me to speak the truth in love, give me the words to say. If you want me to take a stand, stand with me. Guide me and show me what to do. Give me your strength to do what needs to be done.
>
> In Jesus' name,
> Amen

Do not spread warnings unless you have more to go on than just a funny feeling in your gut. As it turns out, "funny feelings" are often nothing but jealousy or selfish ambition.

Need a Body Bag?

I love the bumper sticker that says, "If you can smile when things go wrong, then you must have someone to blame."

Perhaps you've been playing the blame game a lot lately, and maybe for good reason. Maybe you've got a long list of how others have wronged you.

Believe me, I've been there.

One day when I was reviewing a list of offenses I held against a friend I'll call Milly, the Lord suddenly asked me, "Do you want to forgive her?"

I said, "Well, yes, but . . . you have to understand all that Milly did to me."

God responded, "I didn't ask you what Milly did to you, I asked you if you wanted to forgive her."

That's when I realized God was giving me a choice. Yes, Milly had offended me. I could hang on to those offenses and stay miserable, or I could let go. I said to the Lord, "Yes, I *do* want to forgive Milly."

"Okay," the Lord said, and suddenly I was flooded with relief and the knowledge that the offenses I'd carried had evaporated into thin air. I was flooded with sweet freedom. Today, Milly and I have renewed our friendship and I hold no grudge against her. But this did not happen through my power, it happened through the Lord's power when I said yes to a simple question, "Do you want to forgive her?"

I have to admit that there have been other times I've battled hard to forgive another, praying prayers like, "Lord, I've come to you with this grudge before, but I still feel red-hot anger at Suzie Q. Her actions have hurt me and continue to do so. I have already chosen to forgive her, yet I still feel angry. Help! This is bigger than I am. I need your power."

In times like these, there seems to be a battle between my will and my emotions. But still I press in, I press on, and I pray for help as often as I need to. My feelings can take a while to settle down, but when I will myself to forgive, through God's power, my feelings eventually catch up with my resolve.

Patsy Clairmont says in her book *Dancing Bones*,

> I write this at a time when I am trying to break free from resentment and to forgive someone who has hurt me deeply. I've learned that pride can bind us to bitterness, and given time, bitterness will defile our motives and disrupt our health. I'm reminded that forgiving another person doesn't make that individual right, but it will release us from the foothold of the enemy and the acidic qualities of resentment. . . . The valley isn't easy or fair. Justice comes later, after Christ's return. We shouldn't expect ease and fairness to permeate our existence until we hear the trump of God at Christ's return.[3]

Patsy makes good points. Bitterness is bad for our emotions and health. We don't forgive because those who wronged us deserve it. Rather, we forgive because we need to stop carrying a heart full of stones.

It's better to give these stones up to the Lord. He will be happy to carry your burdens for you.

Perhaps it's time to pull out the old body bag. There's one just under your chair. You may not be able to "see" it, but reach for it and unzip it anyway. We're about to fill it up, not with *real* bodies, but figuratively speaking, with those who have wronged you.

All I have to say is it's a good thing these are ever-expanding body bags. This means you can pack as many (figurative) people in your bag as you want. Once your bag is packed, lift it, or if it's too heavy to lift, simply present your bag before the Lord and pray this prayer with me:

Dear Lord,
   I know you've seen how these people have betrayed and hurt me. It wasn't fair or right. But as an act of my will, I am going to lay

these people at your feet. I realize that when I'm carrying a grudge against them, it's just like I am sentenced to dragging them around with me everywhere I go. It's like I'm giving them permission to place a stone in my heart. I want to be free, Lord, not because they deserve it, but because you want me to be free. Therefore, I let go of my grudges. I place these people at the foot of the cross and leave them there with and through your power. I now realize that whatever these people did to me, they did to you. I give you my emotional pain and thank you for setting me free.

> We don't forgive because those who wronged us deserve it. Rather, we forgive because we need to stop carrying a heart full of stones.

In the name of Jesus,
Amen

Good for you! I'm so proud that you prayed this with me. And remember, God has not forgotten you. He sees and loves you. As Max Lucado said, "Others may abandon you, divorce you, and ignore you, but God will love you. Always."[4]

What If You've Betrayed Someone?

James says,

> But if you harbor bitter envy and selfish ambition in your hearts, do not boast about it or deny the truth. Such "wisdom" does not come down from heaven but is earthly, unspiritual, demonic. For where you have envy and selfish ambition, there you find disorder and every evil practice. But the wisdom that comes from heaven is first of all pure; then peace-loving, considerate, submissive, full of mercy and good fruit, impartial and sincere (3:14–17).

Once when I flew to Boston to speak, Heather, my meeting planner, led me to the conference book table where she instructed me to check my books into the conference bookstore. That's when I noticed a change in Heather. She suddenly seemed upset, though I couldn't imagine why.

An unsettled "mood" came over me and stayed with me even after I checked into my hotel room. That night, I was unable to sleep and was startled by a dark presence, a demon, who appeared before me and told me his name.

> Jealousies, gossip, and lies are not harmless. They are not harmless when they are brought against us, and neither are they harmless when we bring them against others.

I didn't wait to hear what else he might say, and bid it leave immediately in the name of Jesus. It did.

But the encounter left me shaken. I cried out to God until I felt his presence. "It's okay now," he finally said at 2:00 a.m.

The next morning, the meeting planner picked me up to drive me to the meeting. "I have to apologize to you," she said. "Last night, when I saw how many books you'd written I became jealous. I was so jealous that I couldn't sleep until I asked Jesus to forgive me."

"What time was that?" I asked.

"About 2:00."

That's how I understood what had happened. Heather's jealousy had somehow caused a rift in the covering of prayer that the conference prayer team had spread over me. I became vulnerable to attack until Heather placed her jealousy under the submission of Christ.

Jealousies, gossip, and lies are *not* harmless. They are not harmless when they are brought against us, and neither are they harmless when we bring them against others.

The Lord taught me that when I am tempted to be jealous of someone else, I am too self-focused. After all, it's not always about me or what I want; rather, it's about a loving God being good to *all* his children. When God gives a gift to someone besides me, I need to recognize that it's either not my turn or this particular gift was never meant to be mine. So, when someone else gets a gift I covet, I need to love both God, the giver of all good gifts, as well as the one who received God's gift, even more than the gift itself.

For example, many years ago I was up to receive a prestigious speaking award. However, the award went to another speaker. I was more than tempted to have a private pity party, but after a bit of reflection, I gave my feelings of jealousy to God. He helped me realize that it simply was not my turn and even if it was never my turn, I could enjoy that my friend got the recognition she deserved.

In fact, I soon discovered the award was just the encouragement my friend needed in a difficult time.

I learned my lesson; instead of focusing on what someone else has, it's comforting to know the Lord trusts me even when I don't get what I want.

If you have trouble with jealousies or selfish ambition, I'd like to ask you to pull out your trash can. You have a few deposits to make.

Dear Lord,

I confess any jealousy, lies, selfish ambition, and gossip to you. Please forgive me! I lay these sins at the foot of the cross. Please replace my feelings of insecurity, anger, bitterness, jealousy, and spite, with your love.

In the name of Jesus,
Amen

Trip to the Oasis

Here's a paraphrase of Psalm 34:11–19 to pray.

I will fear the Lord. For I love life and desire to see many good days, therefore, I will not speak evil or lies. I will turn from evil and speak peace and pursue it.

I know that the eyes of the Lord are on me and that his ears have heard my cries. The face of the Lord is against those who do evil. He will cut off the memory of them from the earth.

When I cry out, the Lord hears me and delivers me from all my troubles. The Lord is close when I am heartbroken or crushed in spirit.

Troubles may appear, but the Lord delivers me from them all.

PRAYER EXPERIENCE

Dear Lord,

Forgive me for my part in the strife that is in my life. Replace my cold love for others with your love. Replace my bitterness with your peace. Replace my selfish ambition with trusting you. Lead me so that I do not fall under the control of my own evil lusts and self-justifications.

Give me your power to forgive and to live in your peace.

In the name of Jesus,

Amen

Continue to pray with me at www.IgniteMyFaith.com, Chapter Videos, then Chapter 6.

7

Praying for Breakthroughs

*Stay with G*OD*! Take heart. Don't quit. I'll say it again: Stay with G*OD.

—Psalm 27:14 The Message

Even after God brought my daughter out of her yearlong coma, I had a hard time accepting her paralysis and disabilities. I believed the only solution was a healing miracle. After all, I'd already seen God heal my younger brother from paralysis after a horrible car crash left him paralyzed from the neck down. A few months after the crash, he defied all odds and walked out of the rehab center. So a similar miracle for Laura, in my opinion, not only seemed possible, but likely. Anticipating that miracle is the reason I decided to study everything I could on how to pray for healing.

So, when I learned a famous faith healer was coming to Denver, I decided to take my daughter to the service. So, there we sat, Laura in her wheelchair and me sitting next to her, squeezing her little hand. I listened intently as this man of God spoke of the incredible miracles he'd witnessed in Africa; the lame could walk, the blind could see. He stopped his message to point at me. "I know why you came here tonight," he said. "You're hoping I will use my faith to pray for a miracle for your daughter. But what you have to understand is this: you already have faith because faith simply believes God is able."

> Often, when we are waiting in prayer for relief, God is waiting in that same prayer for a deeper relationship with us.

He was right. My question wasn't, "Hey, God, are you *able* to heal my daughter?" my question was, "So, God, what's taking so long?"

Perhaps you've had this very same question. Yes, you believe in a God of miracles, you already know God has the power to change your situation. So, your question is, *What is God waiting for?*

I'm not saying that I know the mind of God for your situation, but I do know this: often, when we are waiting in prayer for relief, God is waiting in that same prayer for a deeper relationship with us.

Perhaps the key to the breakthrough you long for is to go deeper into a relationship with the living God.

Going Deeper with God

God is all about relationship. In fact, we were designed to be in relationship with him.

Look at it this way, when you come to faith, God's Holy Spirit enters you. As we mentioned earlier, you truly become his walking, talking temple as 1 Corinthians 3:16 explains: "Don't you know that you yourselves are God's temple and that God's Spirit dwells in your midst?"

So you don't have to go to church to talk to God, you *are* his church. Your life is a sacred place, filled with God's Holy Spirit. So when you talk to God, he can't help but hear you. In fact, he sees and hears everything you say or do. As God's son or daughter, you are already in a relationship with him because the living God has breathed his Holy Spirit into your soul. This is why it's so important to acknowledge his presence. When you understand that he is with you, that changes everything.

Below, I give you my top six suggestions to help you acknowledge his presence in your everyday life.

1. **Worship God**—My number one suggestion to acknowledge God's presence in your life is to learn how to live your life as an act of worship. That means you must stay aware of his presence and live in such a way that you continually acknowledge God as the point and very reason of your existence.

2. **Put on the whole armor of God**—Daily ask God to (1) gird you with truth; (2) robe you with the righteousness of Christ; (3) help you walk in the gospel of peace; (4) shield you with faith; (5) cover your head with salvation; (6) help you pray about everything; (7) help you stay alert to the enemy (Eph. 6:11–18).

3. **Pray for others**—Jesus taught us to "bless those who curse you, pray for those who mistreat you" (Luke 6:28). Impossible? Not when you use the power of God to help you pray. And prayer is of the utmost importance. Francis Frangipane says, "Until the body of Christ learns to pray for one another, we will continually find ourselves being manipulated by demons who exploit the prayerlessness of Christians."[1]

4. **Love God**—Acknowledge your love for God daily!

5. **Love the people God has put in your life**—It's time to make things right with both God and man. Recently I went to a benefit to help raise money for a man who is dying of cancer. Though Joe has only been given a year to live, he stood in front of his friends and family and said these profound words: "Knowing I have a year to live is all good with me. God has given me time to get right with him, to forgive and to be forgiven, and to say good-bye to my loved ones."

These are strong and passionate words that we should all live by, especially considering most of us, unlike Joe, have no idea when we might breathe our last breath.

6. **Trust God**—Trusting God might be harder than believing God is able to change our circumstances. Because when the answer doesn't come when we believe it should, our spirits can become bitter toward God. When this happens, we must confess that bitterness, then ask for God's strength to help us trust that he is indeed moving.

Waiting

As you draw nearer to God, he will draw nearer to you. Drawing near to God is a wonderful way to wait for your breakthrough (James 4:8).

I believe perseverance is a trait that God loves to see in us. Paul explains in Philippians 3:12–14, "But I press on to take hold of that for which Christ Jesus took hold of me. Brothers and sisters, I do not consider myself yet to have taken hold of it. But one thing I do: Forgetting what is behind and straining toward what is ahead, I press on toward the goal to win the prize for which God has called me heavenward in Christ Jesus."

Why does God value perseverance? I believe it's because perseverance transforms us. Consider the nation of Israel as they pressed on through the desert after escaping from Egypt. Francis Frangipane says, "In the relatively short period of forty years, the Lord transformed a nation that had known only slavery for hundreds of years; he made them into a mighty army feared by all the nations."[2]

> When you understand that God is with you, that changes everything.

God wants us to be transformed into a mighty army, a people who no longer fear our enemy but trust in God as we follow his lead into a land of promises.

Breakthrough!

I like this quote by American humorist Arnold Henry Glasgow: "Nothing lasts forever, not even your troubles."[3]

This is good news. And it's true, our lives are made up, for the most part, of temporary seasons. The things we worried about twenty years ago, or even last week for that matter, may no longer be in our thoughts. One reason is because time marches on and the things we worried about as children may no longer matter in our grown-up world. Another reason our worries disappear is because as we pray over our issues, God answers. Adoniram Judson, a missionary to Burma two hundred years ago, once said, "I never prayed sincerely for anything but that it came. At some time, no matter how distant a day, somehow, in some shape—probably the last I should devise—it came."[4]

To illustrate that God answers those who persevere in prayer, Jesus told this parable:

> In a certain town there was a judge who neither feared God nor cared what people thought. And there was a widow in that town who kept coming to him with the plea, "Grant me justice against my adversary."

For some time he refused. But finally he said to himself, "Even though I don't fear God or care what people think, yet because this widow keeps bothering me, I will see that she gets justice, so that she won't eventually come and attack me!"

And the Lord said, "Listen to what the unjust judge says. And will not God bring about justice for his chosen ones, who cry out to him day and night? Will he keep putting them off? I tell you, he will see that they get justice, and quickly." (Luke 18:2–8)

This is good news! Not only is God *not* unjust, he answers our prayers because he loves us (not because he tires of hearing us whine). But we must continue to seek him. As we seek him, we should believe that he hears us and that he is working it all out for our good (see Rom. 8:28).

While we wait for our breakthrough, we should continue to empty ourselves by continuing to give God our hearts, pride, sins, lives, envy, strife, stress, fear, doubts, confusion, troubles, worries, and more. It's when we pour ourselves out before God that he will increase the oil of his presence in our lives.

This reminds me of the story of the woman who finally got the breakthrough she needed. You see, her husband died, leaving the family in debt. In those days, creditors could sell family members into slavery to pay off what was owed to them. In fact, the deceased husband's creditors were planning to trade this man's two sons into cash at the slave market in town. That's when this widow sought the prophet Elisha's help. Upon learning of her troubles, Elisha quizzed her to discover the only thing she owned was a small jar of olive oil. That's when Elisha called on her to pour it out. Can you imagine? But first, Elisha asked her to gather all the empty jars she could find from both her house and the neighbors, then he instructed her to pour the oil from the small jar into the empty vessels.

So she did as she was told. Her sons kept bringing jars to her, and she filled one after another. Soon every container was full to the brim!

"Bring me another jar," she said to one of her sons.

"There aren't any more!" he told her. And then the olive oil stopped flowing.

When she told the man of God what had happened, he said to her, "Now sell the olive oil and pay your debts, and you and your sons can live on what is left over." (2 Kings 4:5–7 NLT)

When you pour yourself out in prayer and obedience, God will answer and fill you with himself.

When I look back at that day more than twenty years ago, when I was waiting to see if the evangelist would use his faith to heal my daughter, I smile. No, I did not see my daughter rise and walk that day; in fact, I may not see this feat until God transfers us both to heaven. But yet I got the breakthrough I needed, though it was not the breakthrough I'd sought. As I continued to press into God, I learned to pour out my pride, presumption, fear, doubt, and other sins. I learned to worship God, love him, follow him, and obey him. And then one day, I realized the miracle. I had thought God would heal my daughter's broken body but instead he healed my broken heart. I have found his joy and strength, and in so doing, like the Israelites, I've followed God into the Promised Land.

> It's when we pour ourselves out before God that he will increase the oil of his presence in our lives.

If you keep pressing into God, you too will find your break-through. And who knows, it may be exactly the one you requested. But if you're like me, you may find that God's breakthrough will come in disguise. But regardless, it will be a gift of love from God to you. You really can trust God through it all, as we will discuss in the following chapter.

Trip to the Oasis

Let's pray David's petition to the Lord, as found in Psalm 70.

> Hasten, O God, to save me;
>> come quickly, LORD, to help me.
>
> May those who want to take my life
>> be put to shame and confusion;
>
> may all who desire my ruin
>> be turned back in disgrace.
>
> May those who say to me, "Aha! Aha!"
>> turn back because of their shame.
>
> But may all who seek you
>> rejoice and be glad in you;
>
> may those who long for your saving help always say,
>> "The LORD is great!"
>
> But as for me, I am poor and needy;
>> come quickly to me, O God.
>
> You are my help and my deliverer;
>> LORD, do not delay.

PRAYER EXPERIENCE

Dear Lord,

Help me to draw nearer to you as you draw nearer to me while I wait on you for my breakthrough. Help me to pour myself out in prayer, love, obedience, worship, trust, and warfare as I daily put on the armor of God. In and through you, I put on my helmet of salvation, I wear the righteousness of Jesus as a breastplate, I buckle truth around my waist, I pick up the shield of faith and the sword of prayer. I stand in the shoes of the Good News. So armed, I stand before you, thanking you, praising you, and praying for others as well as for my breakthrough of _____.

In fact, I give you my problem of _____ and ask that you give me your mercy, grace, and favor and lead me to the breakthrough you designed for this situation, according to your will.

In Jesus' name,

Amen

Listen as I make a few closing comments on the subject of strife at www.IgniteMyFaith.com, Chapter Videos, then Chapter 7.

8

Praying the Prayer of Trust

Prayer puts God's work in his hands—and keeps it there.

—E. M. Bounds[1]

Decades ago I attended a sales meeting where a so-called expert brought up an interesting theory. He explained that we could get the universe to bring us anything we wanted simply by programming our minds to expect it. "If you cast what you want to the universe," he'd said, "what you want will come to you."

I had never heard such a message in my life, so I bought the man's book and began to study his so-called "secret." It wasn't long until I realized that this expert was trying to teach me how to believe without having faith in God or seeking his favor. This man's message was nothing more than a lie wrapped in truth. Yes, he made some good points. For example, he explained that when we identify our goals, we can more easily achieve them. This is true! This is the same principle you use when you program an address into a Global Positioning System (GPS). Once you type in the address you wish to find and begin to follow the prompts, you dramatically increase your chances of arriving at your chosen destination. In this same way, when you set a goal and continue to move toward it, you dramatically increase your chances of reaching your goal.

Setting goals is much like how an athlete mentally practices hitting a home run or shooting a perfect basket. In other words, when we focus on goals and mentally prepare to achieve them, we better our chances of doing so. This truth is based on exercising the power of our God-given minds. It is nothing more than the God-created principle of focus.

Counterfeit Faith

This expert stepped out-of-bounds when he taught we should call on the supernatural power of the universe to bring us our heart's desires.

Why is this wrong? For starters, the Word teaches us to call not on creation but on the Creator. We are to call on the supernatural power of God to supply our needs (Phil. 4:19).

We need to honor God. The best way to do that, besides seeking and following him, is by checking our motives of envy or selfish ambition at the door. By doing so, we will be better able to honor God by submitting to his will over our own. But figuring out the difference between our will and God's can be a challenge that requires prayers like:

Lord, you know how much I would love to accomplish _____.
If the desire for this goal is caused by envy or selfish ambition, I ask that you reveal my heart to me. Forgive me. Help me to lay my envy and selfishness down at your feet.

Also, Lord, if this desire isn't your best for me, take it away, for I do not want to venture into these goals without you. But, if this goal is from you, I give you control and ask that you dream it and fulfill it for me through your power. For my first objective is to walk with you.

In the name of Jesus,
Amen

God answers this prayer! When I base my dreams and goals on God's will, miracles happen.

When I pray this kind of prayer, asking God to accompany me, he shows up, he opens doors, and his presence is with me. And regardless of the final outcome, I have nothing to fret over. I've given the results to God. I only want to move forward if God is moving forward before me and with me.

> When I base my dreams and goals on God's will, miracles happen.

Know this: with God as your partner, doors open and you will be able to walk into places through his power. There's no need to be afraid when you walk with God, for you can continue to cast your every care on him, even your fear of the challenges before you.

Roadblocks

But what happens when our challenges turn into roadblocks?

The first thing you need to do is to take your roadblock to God in prayer. Say:

God, I didn't expect to stop progressing toward my goal, nor did I expect the floor to drop out of my situation, but if this is your way of leading me, you have my permission. For I let go of the ownership of this situation and give it to you. Lord, turn this situation into a miracle. In the name of Jesus.

Then, to the enemy say:

I rebuke you in the power of the name of Jesus from this situation. If you are behind this current crisis, you might as well give up. Because what you did or plan to do will only multiply the miracle God will perform. Because what you mean for evil, God means for good (Gen. 50:20). So, in the name of Jesus, back off; your schemes, designs, and assignments over me are broken by the blood of Jesus.

Let's return to the reason why the advice of the "expert" went wrong. The trouble is, when we pray to any power outside of the power of God, we are praying ourselves into a trap. We are inviting non-God power to dance with us, power that is more likely than not demonic power. Did you know that demons are not above manipulating circumstances to bring you what you want? They hate obeying you but will oblige you in order to get what *they* want—the power to hurt you and to separate you from God.

Beware! Do not demand that the power of the universe bring you your heart's desire. Otherwise, you may find the thing you wanted is the thing that will bring you grief and pain. If you don't believe me, go to the grave of any young rock star who summoned demonic power to bring him fame. If he could, he would tell you that though he received the fame he sought, it came at the price of his own destruction.

A woman confided in me, "When I willfully stepped out of God's will and married my dream millionaire, I entered a nightmare. Instead of the happiness I thought could be bought with my riches, I have experienced the poverty of extreme emotional trauma. Going against God wasn't worth it. If I could go back in time, I would trade all I have for a chance to heed God's warning."

The goal of living a life of faith is never to go against God but to go with him. It isn't so much about getting what you want, it's about seeking God's best, then trusting him with his answer. I like how Max Lucado puts it: "Faith is not the belief that God will do what you want. It is the belief that God will do what is right."[2]

Once you "get" this, then your *faith* in God will turn into *trust* in God.

Praying the Prayer of Trust

C. S. Lewis once said, "I gave in, and admitted that God was God."[3] This profound admission is the first step in learning how to trust God. We have to stop trying to be our own all in all and let God be God. We may use prayer to the God of the universe for help with our plans, but in the end, we must honor him by submitting to him. We must let go of whatever control we perceive we have in our life in order to trust him.

> The goal of living a life of faith is never to go against God but to go with him. It isn't so much about getting what you want, it's about seeking God's best, then trusting him with his answer.

A few months ago, I visited the Balcones Springs Conference Center near Austin, Texas. That Saturday afternoon during our free time, the event planner announced that we could zip-line across the lake. I decided I would walk down to the lake to watch. And I have to admit, the women looked like they were having fun. One by one, they put on a helmet and a harness, climbed up a telephone pole, and attached themselves to a cable before jumping off a twenty-foot-high platform to glide across the lake on a wire. They invited me to follow them. When I finally agreed, I was in for a surprise. Little did I know what fear issues would surface as I got ready to jump.

My first problem occurred when I tried to climb up the telephone pole. Though I was on belay, meaning I was wearing a harness attached to a rope held fast by the zip-line master, I had more than a bit of difficulty climbing up the pegs attached to the telephone pole. I could imagine the person who had positioned these removable pegs. He was young, athletic, and lanky, unlike me, who was feeling old, plump, and extremely short. The pegs were placed so far apart that my attempts to lift my foot high enough to reach the next peg generally resulted in me kicking that peg off the pole. But each time a peg fell off, one of my young and faithful friends managed to scale up the pole to replace it so I could continue my climb. But the final stretch from the pole to the platform was almost too much. It took a lot of prayer and patience on the part of my (did I mention young?) girlfriends before I could make the final shimmy and stretch. By the time I sat on the platform and clipped myself to the wire stretching across the lake, I was traumatized. But no one seemed to notice. These young and beautiful women merely smiled and said, "Okay, Linda, jump."

They apparently couldn't hear my pounding heart or else they never would have asked me to jump off a twenty-foot cliff as if they were inviting me to tea. To compound matters, my mother's voice began to play through my mind, "So, Linda, if all your friends were to jump off a cliff, would you jump too?"

I looked down and frowned. Suddenly, I wasn't so sure that I could jump. But I was positive I couldn't climb back down the telephone pole. I concluded that I didn't have a choice. I had to make a leap of faith.

I felt beads of sweat pop out on my brow as I tried to psych myself up for the vault. I'd looked down at the lake below and swayed in time with the women's count, "One, two, three . . . jump!"

I froze.

They repeated the count, "One, two, three . . . jump!"

Nothing.

Finally, the zip-line master suggested, "Stop looking down. Close your eyes and push off the edge of the platform just like you were pushing toward God."

I nodded, closed my eyes, and recited the now-familiar chant with the women below, "One, two, three . . . jump!"

And I did! Suddenly, I found myself gliding as the wind fingered through my hair. I opened my eyes and discovered total bliss as the peaceful lake rushed beneath me. Soon, I fell into the waiting arms on the platform on the other side of the lake. I'd done it. I had zip-lined across the lake.

Trusting God is a lot like jumping off a cliff. It's hard to do when you're focusing on your fears. You have to close your eyes and trust God as you let go.

To commemorate my jump, I paraphrased Psalm 23.

> The Lord is my zip-line master.
> I shall not want to scream.
> He makes me to harness up in the green pastures.
> He leads me to glide over still waters.
> He restores my soul.
> He leads me up telephone poles of righteousness for his
>   name's sake.
> Yeah, though I fling myself through the valley of the
>   shadow of death,
> I will not fear falling.
> For you are belaying me.

Your ropes and clips, they comfort me.
You prepare a launchpad before me
in the presence of both friends and enemies.
You anoint my hair with wind.
My endorphins runneth over.
Surely other zip-liners will follow me—
all the days of my life.
And I will glide in the afternoons
with the Lord—forever.

My experience makes me think of Proverbs 3:5, which says, "Trust in the LORD with all your heart and lean not on your own understanding." And that's it! Forget the trouble you see before you, don't listen to the voices that try to stop you; instead, focus on God and go where he leads.

Another important component in trusting God is recognizing that our goals may not always be in tune with God's. I've mentioned this before, but it's such an important concept, bear with me as I bring it back to your attention.

It's hard to imagine that our solutions to life's dilemmas may not be the same as God's solutions. But Isaiah 55:8–9 puts it like this: "'For my thoughts are not your thoughts, neither are your ways my ways,' declares the LORD. 'As the heavens are higher than the earth, so are my ways higher than your ways and my thoughts than your thoughts.'"

> When you begin to believe that God loves you, it becomes easier to trust him and much easier to wait on him.

My friend Gracie explained it this way: "I always thought that losing my job would be the absolute worst thing that could even happen to me until that Friday afternoon when my manager gave me my pink slip. I went home and pouted, wondering, 'What could God be thinking?'

"I mean, didn't he understand that I needed my job to live?"

Gracie smiled. "But yet, now that I am without a job, I have to tell you that I marvel at God's provision. I am starting to understand that he really does love me. I don't think I would have learned this lesson as deeply as I have if I'd never lost my job and never had the opportunity to see God provide for me in so many faithful ways."

Understanding God's great love for us is another step in learning how to trust God. Margaret Feinberg summed up what it feels like to understand God's love for us when she said,

> When God echoes I love you, it's not a slice of information but a feast of transformation. I am invited to experience the fullness of God's love in my heart, life, and spirit. The holy metamorphosis is designed to ring so genuine and true that others can't help but notice. When I love you is alive in my heart, I become freer to love others. When I love you is alive in my mind, I become better at expressing that love. When I love you is alive in my life, I become a smidgen closer to who God has called and created me to be.[4]

I would add, when I love you is alive in my spirit, it's easier to trust the one who loves me.

Waiting on God

When you begin to believe that God loves you, it becomes easier to trust him and much easier to wait on him. E. M. Bounds said,

> I think Christians fail so often to get answers to their prayers because they do not wait long enough on God. They just drop down and say a few words, and then jump up and forget it and expect God to answer them. Such praying always reminds me of the small boy ringing his neighbor's doorbell, and then running away as fast as he can go.[5]

That's such a great image. How many times do we think that if our prayers aren't answered instantly, God isn't going to answer at all? We fail to see that God is calling us to wait on him. Bounds also said,

> Jesus taught that perseverance is the essential element of prayer. Men must be in earnest when they kneel at God's footstool. Too often we get faint-hearted and quit praying at the point when we ought to begin. We let go at the very point where we should hold on strongest. Our prayers are weak because they are not impassioned by an unfailing and resistless will.[6]

Let's stop and plant a prayer seed together, knowing that this seed of prayer will grow as we water it with both our tears and time.

Dearest Lord,

I want to trust you, I do. But sometimes I am so weary in prayer. When things don't go as I expect, I begin to doubt. But Lord, I exchange my doubt for the supernatural ability to trust in you. I come to you just as I am, submitting to your will, and waiting for you to answer my cry. Lord, I know you have heard my prayer. I know that you love me. I know that you are moving as I pray for _____, knowing that my prayers are living in your presence. I water my prayers with my tears and longing for you to answer me. For you are my God, in you I will trust.

In the name of Jesus,
Amen

Do not grow weary in this prayer. Repeat it every time it comes to your mind and heart. Go the distance with God, waiting on him until in his perfect timing you receive your answer.

Letting Go Prayer

It can be hard to let go in absolute surrender and trust God. Like Henry Blackaby teaches, we have to come to a place where we decide if we will ask God to bless what we are doing or instead ask God to help us do what he is blessing. Additionally we even have to decide if we will hold on to our pain or if we will release our pain to God and continue to trust him.

Releasing our pain to God is no easy task. Even the prophet Samuel struggled with letting go of grief. He was brokenhearted when God rejected King Saul because of Saul's disobedience. But one day God spoke to Samuel and said, "How long will you mourn for Saul, since I have rejected him as king over Israel? Fill your horn with oil and be on your way; I am sending you to Jesse of Bethlehem. I have chosen one of his sons to be king" (1 Sam. 16:1).

> It is okay to mourn loss. But even in the bitterest loss, there comes a time when we need to let go and to step toward the future with hope.

It is okay to mourn loss. But even in the bitterest loss, there comes a time when we need to let go and to step toward the future with hope. In time, God will help us move beyond the loss, pain, betrayal, hardship, or heartache.

It may not be easy, but God will be there to help you see there is a future beyond your disappointment.

A friend who had once been a popular author came to me in tears after she lost a contract with her publisher.

"I'm devastated," she told me. "My future in ministry is now uncertain."

I told her, "It's okay to mourn today, but trust God. In the near future he will anoint you to go in a new direction, a direction you wouldn't have taken without this loss. His presence will go with you and guide you."

What I said to her proved true, as she's now happily involved in new ministry opportunities.

How did I know that God would do this for my friend? Because I've seen him move on my behalf when everything went wrong, like the time I got kicked out of seminary.

What did I do to get expelled?

I married my husband, a man who was not a seminary student.

When I received the letter telling me I was no longer a student, I wrote the seminary president and told him that Jesus would not have removed Mary from sitting at his feet just because she was a woman. The president wrote back and said, "We don't want Marys, we want Marthas who will get to work." (Never mind that I was currently working as a youth director.)

I was devastated, especially when the next Sunday I was fired from my church job when the pastor called me to the front of the sanctuary and gave me a plaque to thank me for my work, telling me I would be missed.

What had I done to be fired?

Nothing—it was just that the new pastor wanted to give my job to his best friend, who had just graduated from the same seminary I'd been kicked out of.

I was wounded and angered by these events. But now that I look back on these incidents decades later, I can see that God's hand was at work all along. God had anointed me for a different work, work as a writer and speaker. I'm not sure I would have ever discovered that call if God hadn't removed me from my dream of going to seminary to be a youth worker.

Sure, it hurt. And if I had allowed myself, I could have continually mourned my loss and missed out on moving on with God.

My first breakthrough came when I was invited to write teen devotional books that reached tens of thousands of young people, more young people than I could have reached if I had continued in my work as a youth director. Then came the day when I learned that my former seminary used the book I wrote with Bill Fay—*Share Jesus without Fear*—as a textbook.

Only God could have accomplished that.

I came full circle, and in so doing I saw my books minister to youth and even saw my books go where I could not: to seminary. These events happened, not on my terms, but on God's. Now that I have the gift of hindsight I can tell you that God's ways were better than what I had originally planned.

But I didn't have hindsight when I mourned over losing my place in seminary and losing my job as a youth director. If

> We can know, through faith, that despite any current disappointment we are experiencing, God has a plan that will carry us to the day when we can look back and say, "See, God was moving all along. Praise be to God."

I had, I would have dried my tears a lot sooner; it would have been easier to trust God through these events. But herein lies the difficulty—we are called to trust God *before* we have hindsight. This is a privilege. We can know, through faith, that despite any current disappointment we are experiencing, God has a plan that will carry us to the day when we can look back and say, "See, God was moving all along. Praise be to God."

Trip to the Oasis

It was David who Samuel anointed with his horn of oil to be king. And even though David was anointed by God, he was pursued through hill, valley, and cave by Saul. Here's a prayer David prayed when he was still on the run. Pray it as a prayer of your own.

The enemy pursues me,
    he crushes me to the ground;
he makes me dwell in the darkness
    like those long dead.
So my spirit grows faint within me;
    my heart within me is dismayed.
I remember the days of long ago;
    I meditate on all your works
    and consider what your hands have done.
I spread out my hands to you;
    I thirst for you like a parched land.
Answer me quickly, Lord;
    my spirit fails.
Do not hide your face from me
    or I will be like those who go down to the pit.
Let the morning bring me word of your unfailing love,
    for I have put my trust in you.
Show me the way I should go,
    for to you I entrust my life.
Rescue me from my enemies, Lord,
    for I hide myself in you.
Teach me to do your will,
    for you are my God;
may your good Spirit
    lead me on level ground. (Ps. 143:3–10)

Prayer Experience

Dear Lord,

Please forgive me for the times I got so caught up in my disappointments that I failed to trust in you as I should. Give me your supernatural strength to stop mourning and to be brave enough to step into a new direction with and through you. Heal my broken heart and draw nearer to me than ever. For I belong to you. Lead me, guide me, and help me to trust you through it all.

In Jesus' name,

Amen

Watch my teacup example as I talk about how to pray the prayer of trust at www.IgniteMyFaith, Chapter Videos, then Chapter 8.

9

Praying Prayers of Grace and Favor

From his abundance we have all received one gracious bless-
ing after another.

—John 1:16 NLT

With my busy travel schedule, I've learned the difference between praying for traveling mercies and praying for traveling grace. Praying for mercies always gets me through whatever hair-raising trial comes with the journey, but praying for grace helps me to skip the trial and arrive at my destination without incident.

It's like the time I realized I desperately needed to hire a part-time assistant as soon as the new year rolled around. Trouble was, I had some huge ministry bills I had to pay off before I could consider hiring anyone. When I calculated how much I needed to zero my bills and create a cash reserve for paydays and other ministry needs, I was stunned to see the figure came to a whopping twenty-five-thousand dollars.

My heart sank. As it was almost the second week of December, my publishing and speaking income were over for the year so there was no chance I could raise a buck, much less twenty-five-thousand bucks. The way I figured it, I'd be lucky to pay off my bills by the end of the following year. But I couldn't help but wonder, *If I give God my need for twenty-five-thousand dollars, will he grant me the grace to receive it?*

> Mercy, though crucial, brings us through, but grace adds an extra touch of God's goodness.

I decided to find out and boldly prayed, "Lord, I ask for your grace to raise twenty-five-thousand dollars by Christmas."

I didn't have to wait long to see if God would answer. Though I didn't post my need, my post office box was suddenly flooded with unexpected checks to my ministry. Then three weeks later, on Christmas evening, when I tallied the unexpected giving, I was stunned to discover I had collected twenty-five-thousand dollars and ten cents. Wow!

I was able to pay my debts in full and had enough left to set aside for ministry need and to hire a new assistant.

God's *mercy* was extended to me when God helped me pay my debt. God's *grace* was extended to me when he helped me pay it in record time plus store up a reserve for the new year's expenses.

Did I deserve this kind of mercy or grace?

No, and that's the point. You see, mercy is when God blesses by not giving us what we deserve, but grace is sweeter, as it's the added bonus of undeserved blessings. Mercy, though crucial, brings us through, but grace adds an extra touch of God's goodness.

Once I realized this principle, I began to pray for more of God's grace in my life: family grace, ministry grace, and even bill-paying grace. And it seems to me that God answers my grace requests out of his abundant love.

According to dictionary.com, grace is "the freely given, unmerited favor and love of God; the influence or spirit of God operating in humans to regenerate or strengthen them."[1]

When we pray prayers of grace we are praying for our needs by asking for the unmerited favor and love of God. And the result is that the Spirit of God regenerates and strengthens us by the way he answers these prayers, even when the answer isn't exactly what we had in mind.

But back to my applying this principle of grace to my need for ministry funds. Please note that if God had not answered my prayer with cash, I could still trust that his grace and mercy were abundantly flowing toward me. I know this because I know that God sees the big picture.

When he answers a prayer with a "no" or "wait," he does so because he wants to give us the grace we really need instead of the grace we think we want.

God's Favor

Favor, according to dictionary.com means, "something done or granted out of goodwill, rather than from justice or for remuneration; a kind act: to ask a favor."[2]

That's it! Favor from God is when he does something for us, a kindness, out of his goodwill. Not because we deserve it but because he is a loving God.

The quest for man's favor can go to extremes. In 1873, the mining town of Central City, Colorado, wanted to impress President Ulysses Grant with a tour of their town, which included a tour of one of the local gold mines. So before Grant arrived, the members of the town paved a prominent sidewalk with pure silver bricks,[3] then they loaded their shotguns with gold dust and blasted the walls of the mine until they glittered gold. But the glitter was only for show; as soon as Grant left their fair city, the good townsfolk reclaimed both the silver bricks as well as the gold dust embedded in the mine's walls.

I think a lot of us try to impress God much this same way. We try to make ourselves appear better than we really are. But if we want more of God's favor, we should quit trying to impress God and just love him with our whole hearts.

> **If we want more of God's favor, we should quit trying to impress God and just love him with our whole hearts.**

But the good news is that though none of us are holy or righteous enough to win God's favor, we have God's favor in spite of ourselves. We can find the proof in Luke 2, when the angels sang at the birth of Jesus, "Glory to God in the highest heaven, and on earth peace to those on whom his favor rests" (Luke 2:14).

Jesus himself told us of God's favor when he read from the Scripture in the temple in Nazareth. Unrolling the scroll of Isaiah, he read,

> The Spirit of the Lord is on me, because he has anointed me to proclaim good news to the poor. He has sent me to proclaim freedom for the prisoners and recovery of sight for the blind, to set the oppressed free, to proclaim the year of the Lord's favor. (Luke 4:18–19)

Even now, God's favor rests on us. We know because Paul told the church of the Corinthians, "As God's co-workers we urge you not to receive God's grace in vain. For he says, 'In the time of my favor I heard you, and in the day of salvation I helped you.' I tell you, now is the time of God's favor, now is the day of salvation" (2 Cor. 6:1–2).

But having God's favor does not always mean that our lives are without trial. For Paul proclaimed God's favor despite the trials he and his friends endured.

As servants of God we commend ourselves in every way: in great endurance; in troubles, hardships and distresses; in beatings, imprisonments and riots; in hard work, sleepless nights and hunger; in purity, understanding, patience and kindness; in the Holy Spirit and in sincere love; in truthful speech and in the power of God; with weapons of righteousness in the right hand and in the left; through glory and dishonor, bad report and good report; genuine, yet regarded as impostors. (2 Cor. 6:4–8)

What kind of favor is this? I'm apparently not the only one who wants to know. Just last night I was in a restaurant and overheard a teenage boy discuss a friend with his parents. "I told Shelby, you say that God loves you, but with all you're going through, have you considered that maybe God doesn't?"

Ouch! Be careful not to believe this lie, for the solution to this paradox comes as Paul continues the passage. "Dying, and yet we live on; beaten, and yet not killed; sorrowful, yet always rejoicing; poor, yet making many rich; having nothing, and yet possessing everything" (2 Cor. 6:9–10).

Yes! Only through Christ can one die but live, be beaten down but continue on, have joy through their sorrows, and be rich without wealth.

Maybe this isn't what you signed up for, but as Paul explained, it's about having nothing but possessing everything. So in other words, it's about living in the presence of God.

Living in the Presence of God

Experiencing God's favor doesn't mean you will never have trials; it means you will have God's presence through the trial. Let's review again the conversation Moses had with the Lord in Exodus 33.

After God told Moses to lead his people across the desert, Moses acknowledged God's favor and asked God to continue it.

The Lord replied, "My Presence will go with you, and I will give you rest" (v. 14).

> Only through Christ can one die but live, be beaten down but continue on, have joy through their sorrows, and be rich without wealth.

Here lies the key to experiencing favor. Even in the middle of great difficulty, when we abide with Christ, our hearts can rest in the presence of God. Moses understood this principle and replied, "If your Presence does not go with us, do not send us up from here" (v. 15).

God not only promised Moses that he would abide with him, he promises us as well as we read in 1 John 4: "All who confess that Jesus is the Son of God have God living in them, and they live in God. We know how much God loves us, and we have put our trust in his love" (vv. 15–16 NLT).

And the good news is that God not only has graced us with the favor of his presence, he also has favored us with more promises than I can list.

God's Promises

Take some time to study and to look up the Scripture that accompanies each promise.

God's Word promises that God will:

- answer us (John 15:7)
- comfort us (Ps. 23:4)
- give us courage (Ps. 138:3)
- give us eternal life (John 10:28)
- give us faith (Eph. 2:8)

- be faithful (Josh. 1:9)
- forgive us (John 3:16)
- give us freedom from sin and death (Rom. 8:2)
- guide us (Ps. 48:14)
- heal us (1 Pet. 2:24)
- hear us (Ps. 3:4)
- give us joy (Neh. 8:10)
- never leave us (Heb. 13:5)
- love us (Deut. 23:5)
- give us rest (Matt. 11:28–29)
- give us peace (Phil. 4:7)
- give us power over the enemy (Luke 10:19)
- protect us from the enemy (James 4:7)
- provide for us (Phil. 4:19)
- give us strength (Ps. 18:32)
- relieve our suffering (Mark 5:34)
- give us victory (1 Cor. 15:57)
- give us victory over temptation (James 1:12–16)
- give us wisdom (James 1:5)

That's a pretty impressive list, and a list you can pray through. For example, let's pray through the "give us victory" promise like this:

Dear Lord,

I am asking for grace and favor in victory over _____.
Your Word in John 14:14 says, "You may ask me for anything in my name, and I will do it." Thank you for this promise. I will stand on it in your grace and favor, trusting you for victory over _____.
Please move, and show me how to follow you concerning this.

In Jesus' name,
Amen

My list only scratches the surface of all the promises of God. I recommend that as you read the Word daily, make it a habit to discover and embrace his promises for you. But in the meantime let me ask you a question—what do you think would hinder God from fulfilling his promises?

What Hinders God's Promises?

It's true, there were generations during which God's chosen people were so hindered that they did not see God's promises fulfilled in their lives. We want to learn from their mistakes and avoid anything that might hinder God's work and blessing in our own lives.

I recently met Alex Kendrick at the CLASSeminars Christian Writers Conference in Ghost Ranch, New Mexico, and heard him tell his story about how a little church in the farm country of Albany, Georgia, managed to get into the movie business with successful films such as *Flywheel*, *Facing the Giants*, and *Fireproof*.

Alex Kendrick, who served as Sherwood Baptist Church's media pastor, had a feeling that God was calling him to produce a movie. He decided to talk to his senior pastor, who gave him the okay if he could raise twenty thousand dollars without announcing his financial need from the pulpit. A few weeks later, Alex had twenty-thousand-dollars' worth of checks on his desk, all from individual church members who'd come to him saying, "God told me to give this to you."

Using a video camera and setup that he'd purchased on the internet, Alex and his volunteer actors worked afternoons and weekends to film the movie.

Alex said, "I didn't know what I was doing. I didn't even know what to say on the set, so instead of saying 'Action!' I'd say, 'Go.'"

With the film still in editing, Alex approached the manager of the local theater and asked him if he would play it at the theater. The manager checked with his corporate office, and they agreed, saying, "At least the people from the church will come."

That first night at the theater, Alex brought his video projector and pressed play to a packed-out house. The next night, the theater sold out again. When the manager saw the crowds, he told Alex, "Out of our sixteen theaters, you were the second-highest-grossing movie. Do you want to stay another week?"

The movie, *Flywheel*, ended up staying six weeks and grossing thirty-seven-thousand dollars. Later it sold ten thousand copies in a month when they opened the sales at the church. Shortly thereafter, Blockbuster discovered it and distributed it to their stores around the country.

For their next film, Alex and his brother Stephen once again raised the money, this time $100,000, without taking the need to the church. Their new movie, *Facing the Giants*, was about how to face personal giants, told through a story about football. However, it appeared that *Facing the Giants*, unlike *Flywheel*, was out of luck in terms of finding an audience. That is, until Alex gave the control of the movie back to God. Then, through a series of miracles, Sony distributed *Facing the Giants* to 441 screens throughout the country, with ticket sales totaling $10.1 million.

> It's true, there were generations where God's chosen people were so hindered that they did not see God's promises fulfilled in their lives. We want to learn from their mistakes and avoid anything that might hinder God's work and blessing in our own lives.

When it came time to consider creating a new movie, Alex sought God's direction for an entire year until God gave him the idea for the movie *Fireproof*. At their casting call, Alex asked each candidate, including veteran actor Kirk Cameron, the question, "Is there anything in your life that would prevent God from blessing your role in this movie?"

Some people said yes, and dropped out of the project, but others, including Kirk, felt right with God and continued forward. Then, in 2008, *Fireproof* came out and grossed $33.5 million. But besides the fact that the movie was the top independent movie of the year, the companion book, *Love Dare*, hit the *New York Times* Bestsellers list, and helped to restore marriages around the world.[4]

After all these miracles, I'd say that Alex has learned a thing or two about seeking God's favor. He encourages the rest of us to do the same by asking the Lord:

1. Give me your ideas and goals instead of my ideas and goals.
2. Rebuke or stop me if I'm doing anything to prevent your favor.
3. Help me find you as I desperately seek you.

You can see Alex explaining these prayer principles at www .IgniteMyFaith.com, Chapter Videos, then Chapter 9. Alex's prayer ideas will help us root out the sin that hinders. But, you might ask, what kinds of sins will hinder God's favor?

Sins That Hinder

God wants our attention and devotion more than he wants our accomplishments for the kingdom. Otherwise, we've set our devotion to our accomplishments over our devotion to God. When this happens, God himself may become the force that hinders our success. Accomplishments without his Spirit and leading will be empty, lacking both his power and anointing. Therefore, we must carefully avoid worshiping our work and work to abide with Christ.

Let's take a little checkup to see if any of these hindrances are stopping us in our walk and ministry.

Unrepentance

It's a common Bible story. When God's people rebelled, God warned them of coming punishment (see 2 Chron. 19:9–10). Usually this threat brought his people to their knees and back into God's grace. But whenever they refused to repent, they stepped from God's favor and into God's wrath.

> We must carefully avoid worshiping our work and work to abide with Christ.

But God was faithful. Whenever they, or the following generation, repented, God's anger abated and his grace, blessings, and favor returned.

God wants our repentance because one of his many names is *Jealous* (see Exod. 34:14). God is jealous to bring us back under his protection by bringing us back to himself.

Strife

Cain competed with his brother Abel in a contest to worship God. When God accepted Abel's animal sacrifice but rejected Cain's fruit offering, Cain decided to eliminate his competition by killing his brother (see Gen. 4:8). The sin of murder is still the root of strife. We need to call on the supernatural power of God to help us remove this hindrance from our walk with him.

Fear

David, in Psalm 34:4, said, "I sought the LORD, and he heard me, and delivered me from all my fears" (KJV).

God used the trauma David endured while on the run from King Saul to show David that he could be trusted to deliver him. This trust set David free of the hindrance of fear.

Envy and Selfish Ambition

Isaiah 66:2 quotes God as saying, "These are the ones I look on with favor: those who are humble and contrite in spirit, and who tremble at my word." Humility may bring favor, but envy and selfish ambition hinder it. If you see this dynamic duo in you, confess it and ask God to help you overcome.

Oppression

Yes, the devil will hinder you from your breakthrough whenever he can, but there's a wonderful way to stop him, as we've already noted. James 4:7–8 says, "Submit yourselves, then, to God. Resist the devil, and he will flee from you. Come near to God and he will come near to you."

According to Strong's Greek and Hebrew Dictionary, the word *submit* is the Greek work *hupotasso*, which means to subordinate or to obey. So, in other words, we are to come under God's divine leadership in obedience so that Satan will flee. For when we come near to God, he comes near to us.

Doubt and Confusion

Many hindrances to God's promises are related to doubt and confusion. Confusion shows up when we doubt God. It hinders our ability to move with God (see James 1:6–8). But the good news is that confusion is easily remedied by asking God for wisdom (see James 1:5).

Doubt is the fog that clouded the minds of the Israelites when they reached the border of the land God had promised to give them. Doubt filled the hearts of the men who were sent to spy out the land. Though these spies knew the promise of God, though they saw the land God promised them flowed with milk and honey, they brought a bad report that struck fear into the hearts of God's people. In essence, they said, "Those who dwell in the land are giants. Compared to them, we are but grasshoppers" (Num. 13:33).

> Being smaller than the task before us is by God's design so that we will learn we can only go ahead not in our own power but his power.

Why was it that this report stopped God's people from getting their breakthrough? Being smaller than the task before us is by God's design so that we will learn we can only go ahead not in our own power but his power. That's how we become undefeatable; we go as Team God, and by that I mean we go with and through God.

But the Israelites forgot this principle. Never mind that two of the spies, Caleb and Joshua, tore their clothes and begged the people to believe in God and all he had promised. "Only do not rebel against the LORD. And do not be afraid of the people of the land, because we will devour them. Their protection is gone, but the LORD is with us. Do not be afraid of them" (Num. 14:9).

But the children of Israel would not listen. They believed the report of "can't" over the report of "yes we *can* with God."

When we come to a place where we doubt God, where we refuse to move because we are afraid of the giants before us, it becomes impossible to take the land God has promised us. If we refuse to go forth or to obey God, we have hindered his blessing. We have to remember that when we walk with Christ, the answer to the question of doubt is, "Yes, I can with God."

Presumption

The hindrance of presumption occurs when we set ourselves above God, thinking he should obey us because we, after all, have the faith we need to make God perform. We believe he is able so we demand that he give us our own way. However, it's not our place to be God's boss. We can't control God, and it's not our place to try. Instead, we should come to him humbly. We should pray like Jesus prayed in the Garden of Gethsemane before he was crucified for our sins. "My Father, if it is not possible for this cup to be taken away unless I drink it, may your will be done" (Matt. 26:42).

Sometimes God has a greater will than our prayers allow. Even when we don't understand the why, we can still trust that God is moving to turn our situation into a miracle.

Prayerlessness

As I've been gearing up my ministry, seeking God harder than ever and working my way through spiritual warfare, I can tell you that it's such a privilege to go to God with any and every need. There have been times in my life when I did not practice this privilege as I should have. How I missed out on abiding with Christ, realizing his presence, and resting and trusting in him.

Anne Graham Lotz in her book *I Saw the Lord* explains prayerlessness as pride.

Additionally Anne names a few more sins that hinder. She says,

> My exaggeration is lying as it inflates and distorts the truth to make it sound more impressive . . .
>
> My worry is unbelief as it frets over things instead of trusting You completely, even when I don't understand why . . .
>
> My gossip is stealing as it robs another person of his or her reputation . . .[5]

Pray through any and all hindrances to God's favor. As you pray, God, in his great mercy, grace, and favor, will show you other hindrances. Don't ignore them but submit them to him. Remove any and every barrier you can so that you can not only experience God's favor but learn how to more closely abide with him.

> Sometimes God has a greater will than our prayers allow. Even when we don't understand the why, we can still trust that God is moving to turn our situation into a miracle.

Trip to the Oasis

In Psalm 34, David praises God after using his wits to retreat from his foe Abimelech by pretending to be crazy. But this prayer of thanksgiving, trust, and grace is a great prayer to pray anytime, like right now.

> I will bless the LORD at all times;
> His praise *shall* continually *be* in my mouth.
> My soul shall make its boast in the LORD;
> The humble shall hear *of it* and be glad.
> Oh, magnify the LORD with me,
> And let us exalt His name together.
> I sought the LORD, and He heard me,
> And delivered me from all my fears.
> They looked to Him and were radiant,
> And their faces were not ashamed.
> This poor man cried out, and the LORD heard *him,*
> And saved him out of all his troubles.
> The angel of the LORD encamps all around those who fear
>   Him,
> And delivers them.
> Oh, taste and see that the LORD *is* good;
> Blessed *is* the man *who* trusts in Him!

Oh, fear the LORD, you His saints!
> *There is* no want to those who fear Him.

The young lions lack and suffer hunger;
> But those who seek the LORD shall not lack any good
> > *thing.*

Come, you children, listen to me;
> I will teach you the fear of the LORD.

Who *is* the man *who* desires life,
> And loves *many* days, that he may see good?

Keep your tongue from evil,
> And your lips from speaking deceit.

Depart from evil and do good;
> Seek peace and pursue it.

The eyes of the LORD *are* on the righteous,
> And His ears *are open* to their cry. (vv. 1–15 NKJV)

PRAYER EXPERIENCE

Dear Lord,

I ask that you teach me how to have more of your presence in my life. I ask that you anoint my life with your grace, in every circumstance, and that as you do, help me to see and understand that your presence is with me. I also ask for your great favor. If there is anything I am doing to prevent your favor, I ask that you open my eyes and show me with your spirit of truth. I ask that you give me the power to supernaturally rid my life of unrepentance, strife, fear, envy and selfish ambition, oppression (or allowing the enemy to have power over me), doubt and confusion, presumption, and prayerlessness. In addition, I confess and repent of exaggeration, worry, gossip, and lies.

I confess all these sins to you, and I turn from them. I also confess any other thing you may be revealing to me that is standing in the way of your favor, including: _____.

Please forgive me and help me to supernaturally turn from these sins and learn how to more fully rest in your presence, joy, and love as you anoint me with your grace and favor.

In Jesus' name,

Amen

10

Praying for Hope and Healing

We are all faced with a series of great opportunities brilliantly disguised as impossible situations.

—Charles Swindoll[1]

I was sharing my daughter's story with a group of women in Myrtle Beach when I said. "Today my daughter has severe disabilities, and do you know what I have to say about that? I say, *so*? So what? My daughter is happy, and we love her. Besides, who among us doesn't have some sort of disability?"

At the conclusion of my talk, I joined a small discussion group where a mother of a child with autism shared her heartbreak. "I'm furious," Taylor Ann said. "When I took my beautiful two-year-old for her shots, she was normal, walking and talking. I asked the doctor, 'Do you think there's a chance these shots could cause autism?'

"'Not at all,' the doctor assured me."

She batted a tear off her cheek. "But my daughter had an apparent reaction and became autistic overnight. Two years later, she's still autistic. Every time I look at her, I remember the way she was before the autism and I'm furious. But after what Linda shared, it's made me think through my response to my little girl. I've decided to declare this: my daughter is autistic. But *so*? She's my daughter, and I love her. Of course I'm going to continue to pray for her to get better. But here in this moment, when it comes to my daughter's disability, I accept my child, disabilities and all."

> Here's what God wants. He wants you to look up. He wants you to trust him.

Yes, Taylor Ann's daughter is disabled, but her daughter is not her disability. Despite this child's problems, she's still Taylor Ann's little girl and Taylor Ann is still her loving mom. And God is still a God who cares and who can be trusted, even in the face of autism.

Maybe you can relate to this story because you've also experienced terrible disappointment concerning your circumstances. I understand how you feel. I too have struggled through pain to my own personal breakthrough. I've told my story in many venues, but it's such a key to how I've made it through my difficulties that I want to share it with you now.

Four years after the accident, when I began to realize God was not going to give my daughter the healing I'd fought so desperately to receive, I collapsed with grief, climbed into bed, and pulled up my covers and wept. "I've lost all hope," I whispered to the Lord.

Somehow I managed to get to church that night, and the pastor said, "The Lord showed me that someone who had lost all hope was coming."

I shrank in my chair, hoping the pastor wouldn't recognize my guilt. He continued, "Here's what God wants. He wants you to look up. He wants you to trust him."

I have to admit, I was stunned that the Lord had spoken to the pastor about me, but at the same time I was disappointed in the message. I mean, why couldn't the message have been, "You just need to be more patient because soon your daughter will be as good as new"?

I pouted all the way home, not sure I could face my daughter's future if her long list of disabilities was permanent. When I pulled my van into my garage I began to understand the fullness of God's message to me. While I'd been busy trying to have faith in my faith in order to make God do what I wanted, God was waiting for me to totally trust him. It was in that moment I gave in. I gave up trusting in my own faith and began to trust in God no matter what. It was in that moment that God did the greatest miracle of my life—he healed my broken heart.

Perhaps you too are holding on to a vision instead of holding on to God. If that's true, then you're in great company, which includes the prophet Elijah. Elijah hid in the caves of Mount Horeb to escape the wrath of Queen Jezebel. Never mind that he had just experienced God's mighty power as God had sent flames to consume the offering Elijah had laid before him. Never mind that upon witnessing this miracle, Elijah's people had risen to kill all 450 of the queen's false prophets.

Yet, after such a great miracle of God, Elijah was disappointed. Not only was he in fear for his life, he was disappointed that his vision for revival had not been fulfilled. Though the people had risen up to rid their land of Baal worship, they had not risen up to worship the Lord. Consequently, Elijah felt alone, vulnerable, and discouraged. His vision for revival had failed him. But it was at Horeb that he traded his vision for God himself.

Horeb seems to be a common meeting place between people of faith and the Lord. In fact, God met Moses there a second time to reveal himself. But because God's glory was too great for Moses to see, God hid Moses in a rock as he passed by. Moses never saw God coming, but he saw that he had been there.

This is much the same in our lives. God hides us in the rock of Jesus because it's only through God's Son that we can experience God's glory. We don't always see God coming into our circumstances, but when we look back, we can see that he's been there.

But like Moses and Elijah, God is not going to leave us on the mountain; he's going to ask us to follow him into the deserts and valleys as he takes us on a journey of destiny. The more we trust and follow God, the sooner we will cross our deserts and walk through the valleys that lie before us, and the sooner we will see the Promised Land.

But before we get started on our journey, we have to trade our vision for God's vision, as well as his presence.

What to Do When You Lose Hope

While our difficulties may lead us to God, the vision of what we want from God may be the barrier that keeps us from experiencing God himself. In fact, I think God would give us what we ask for more often if we weren't seeking blessings, gifts, or requests more than we were seeking him. Look at it this way—what if you had a friend who never wanted to spend time with you except to demand favors? You might describe your relationship by saying, "I'm her friend, but she's not been a friend to me."

So why do we sometimes come to God with the attitude, "If you love me, you will do what I say. If you care, you will bless me. If you want to be my friend, you will change my situation."

It's like we think we can blackmail God by dangling our friendship as a carrot to get him to do what we want. But what would happen if we prayed instead, "I invite you into my situation, Lord. Bless me with your presence. I trust you completely with my circumstances."

These kinds of prayers will not only change our situation but our lives. Perhaps it would help to pray:

Dear Lord,

    I bring you my vision of _____. But I seek you over my vision. I ask you to move in me as you move on my behalf. I invite you into this situation now. I trust you completely.

In Jesus' name,
Amen

When you finally come to the point where you can pray this kind of prayer, you will find hope and rest in God.

The best ways to find hope are to

- pray
- read the Word
- seek God's voice

> We don't always see God coming into our circumstances, but when we look back, we can see that he's been there.

Pray

I met a woman named Amanda Lynn who was going through a bitter divorce. She'd already burned up one fax machine trying to send her attorney proof that her husband had cheated her in every way. She was angry that her husband had slandered her in court, and she was furious that the money she had brought into her marriage was in jeopardy. She'd already fired one attorney and couldn't stop brooding about her injustice. Finally she sank to her knees and prayed, "Lord, I give you my bitterness, I give you my rights. I give my case to you and leave it at your feet."

That's the moment God stepped into her situation. That's the moment she found freedom from her pain and trauma. She stood and proclaimed, "I'm free!"

To Amanda, it was no longer about battling for her money; it was about walking with and trusting the Lord no matter what.

Read the Word

Today's church often lacks the ability to believe. I think this is because we don't read the Word as we should. This is tragic because the Word has the power to strengthen both our hope and faith. Romans 10:17 says, "Consequently, faith comes from hearing the message, and the message is heard through the word about Christ."

Here are ten of my favorite hope-building Scripture passages. Read each one carefully because there will be a test.

1. "So do not fear, for I am with you; do not be dismayed, for I am your God. I will strengthen you and help you; I will uphold you with my righteous right hand" (Isa. 41:10).
2. "Call to me and I will answer you and tell you great and unsearchable things you do not know" (Jer. 33:3).
3. "Therefore we do not lose heart. Though outwardly we are wasting away, yet inwardly we are being renewed day by day. For our light and momentary troubles are achieving for us an eternal glory that far outweighs them all. So we fix our eyes not on what is seen, but on what is unseen, since what is seen is temporary, but what is unseen is eternal" (2 Cor. 4:16–18).
4. "Trust in the LORD with all your heart and lean not on your own understanding; in all your ways submit to him, and he will make your paths straight" (Prov. 3:5–6).

5. "And we know that in all things God works for the good of those who love him, who have been called according to his purpose" (Rom. 8:28).

6. "Come to me, all you who are weary and burdened, and I will give you rest. Take my yoke upon you and learn from me, for I am gentle and humble in heart, and you will find rest for your souls. For my yoke is easy and my burden is light" (Matt. 11:28–30).

7. "For I know the plans I have for you," declares the LORD, "plans to prosper you and not to harm you, plans to give you hope and a future. Then you will call on me and come and pray to me, and I will listen to you. You will seek me and find me when you seek me with all your heart. I will be found by you," declares the LORD, "and will bring you back from captivity" (Jer. 29:11–14).

> I think God would give us what we ask for more often if we weren't seeking blessings, gifts, or requests more than we were seeking him.

8. "The Lord is near. Do not be anxious about anything, but in every situation, by prayer and petition, with thanksgiving, present your requests to God. And the peace of God, which transcends all understanding, will guard your hearts and your minds in Christ Jesus" (Phil. 4:5–7).

9. "I have learned to be content whatever the circumstances. I know what it is to be in need, and I know what it is to have plenty. I have learned the secret of being content in any and every situation, whether well fed or hungry, whether living in plenty or in want. I can do all this through him who gives me strength" (Phil. 4:11–13).

10. "He who began a good work in you will carry it on to completion until the day of Christ Jesus" (Phil. 1:6).

Seek God's Voice

If you are currently in crisis, please don't beat yourself up if you can't "feel" or "hear" God. Sometimes shock or grief can blind our spiritual eyes and close our spiritual ears. In times like these, we have to take everything we know to be true about God and his love for us on faith—and perhaps that's the point.

But, if you're a God seeker, don't be too sure you haven't heard his voice. Have you ever felt your heart leap upon hearing the Word or an anointed teaching? Have you ever felt his presence when you've spent time in nature, which is forever in worship? Have you ever felt his love or experienced his peace or felt his gentle encouragement? If you can answer yes to any of these questions, then you've heard God's voice.

> Sometimes shock or grief can blind our spiritual eyes and close our spiritual ears. In times like these, we have to take everything we know to be true about God and his love for us on faith—and perhaps that's the point.

When I was a child, it was not uncommon for me to hear adults at church use the phrase "God told me."

I would look at these grownups in awe, marveling that God had spoken to them. It wasn't until I began to desperately seek the Lord on behalf of my daughter that I began to understand that God's voice *could* be heard. I've discovered that the best way to hear his voice is to read his Word—for his Word speaks directly to our hearts. I've also learned I can tune in to his still small voice, which sometimes comes as a gentle whisper, a word, a thought, a dream, or even a vision. Today, when I hear him, I notice he never goes against Scripture, ever. Any voice that does so is not God's. I've also found it's important to test the spirit. On hearing his voice, I ask, "Are you the Lord whose Son died for my sins?" Then I wait for the answer. I've discovered the voice of the enemy will flee before such a question, for 1 John 4:1–3 says,

> Dear friends, do not believe every spirit, but test the spirits to see whether they are from God, because many false prophets have gone out into the world. This is how you can recognize the Spirit of God: Every spirit that acknowledges that Jesus Christ has come in the flesh is from God, but every spirit that does not acknowledge Jesus is not from God. This is the spirit of the antichrist, which you have heard is coming and even now is already in the world.

I've actively practiced listening for God's voice for over twenty years. I've asked questions and waited on him. I've meditated on the Word as it spoke to me. I've sat quietly before him as I recognized his abiding presence and listened. I've learned to practice discernment, separating the voice of my own ego and the whispers of the enemy from the voice of God. I'm not ashamed to tell you that I've learned to recognize him when he speaks. Hearing God's voice takes practice. But then, maybe my difficulties gave me the ability to hear. For if I'd never needed to hear his voice, I wonder if I would have tried so hard to listen.

If you are ready to practice hearing his voice, you're ready for this practice exercise. Choose one of the ten hope Scriptures listed previously and meditate on it. By that, I mean, read it slowly, letting the words seep into your soul. Reread it, then read it yet again. Finally, ask the Lord, "Is there anything you would say to me?"

Listen quietly.

You may feel his presence and love. You may hear his gentle voice of love and encouragement, or you may hear only the sound of your beating heart. Whatever happens, know this is a training exercise. Spend some time every day seeking his voice, and soon you will be certain that you have heard it.

Defeating the Voice of Doubt

Be careful to shut out the voice of doubt. It comes in whispers like:

- God is against you.
- God doesn't love you.
- God doesn't listen to you.
- God knows your past so he's making you suffer.

These statements are false. These doubts are not from the Lord, and perhaps if you're haunted by such thoughts, it's time that you doubted your doubts. Did you know that when Peter walked across the water toward Jesus, it was doubt that sank him? "Immediately Jesus reached out his hand and caught him. 'You of little faith,' he said, 'why did you doubt?'" (Matt. 14:31).

> I've discovered that the best way to hear his voice is to read his Word—for his Word speaks directly to our hearts.

James explains the dangers of doubt like this: "But when you ask, you must believe and not doubt, because the one who doubts is like a wave of the sea, blown and tossed by the wind. That person should not expect to receive anything from the Lord. Such a person is double-minded and unstable in all they do" (James 1:6–8).

So doubting will not only sink you, it will make you seasick. But what can you do when doubts bombard your mind?

First, choose what you will believe, then say it out loud.

To show you what I mean, I've compiled a list of affirmations that are based on our hope Scriptures from above. Say them aloud, and say them as often as necessary.

1. I recognize God is God (Isa. 41:10).
2. I call upon him. Help me, Lord! (Jer. 33:3).

3. I will not fear (Isa. 43:1).
4. I will trust in God (Prov. 3:5–6).
5. I know that he's working things out for me according to his good purpose (Rom. 8:28–29).
6. I trade my burdens for God's presence and rest (Matt. 11:28–30).
7. I know God's plans for me are good (Jer. 29:11–14).
8. I praise God and thank him in all my circumstances (Phil. 4:6–7).
9. I do everything in his strength (Phil. 4:11–13).
10. I know that God is going to complete the good work he started (Phil. 1:6).

Does God Heal Today?

The answer is yes, of course he does. But is there a secret formula to pray to move God to heal our afflictions?

I don't know about a secret formula, but I do have some healing prayer suggestions, which include:

1. Remove the enemy from the situation through the name and blood of Jesus.
2. Believe God is able to answer your prayers.
3. Take your request to God in the name of Jesus.
4. Trust God with your request.
5. Rejoice that God has heard you and is answering your prayer.

(Read these directions again, but this time as a prayer.)

I've seen God's healing in my life as I've suffered with pain and migraines as a result of food sensitivities. God healed my suffering, and today I live mainly free of pain. What a blessing! But I have to admit, there have been times I've prayed the prayer of healing and have not received the answer I requested. Though I don't understand the why of this, I still trust God and thank him for his goodness.

Let me encourage you not to give up on prayers of healing because of fear of disappointment. You can pray prayers of healing with joy—joy because you have the right to ask God; joy because God hears you; joy because you can trust him. The best thing about praying with joy is that joy brings faith and faith brings miracles.

How to Pray for Others

Do not let fear of disappointment keep you from praying the prayer of healing for others. If you do, you will miss out on opportunities to be used by God. Recently, I met a lady who had a swollen knee. "I fell off my bike," Rita told me.

"May I pray for you?"

"Certainly," she said, and so I prayed for healing. I prayed because it was my privilege to come before the Father and pray. I prayed because my Father loves me and because I knew the Father loves her. As I prayed, I felt his love and good pleasure. When I finished praying, Rita's knee was still swollen, but yet I knew God heard my prayer and touched both of us with his love, and that was enough. I left trusting that God would finish the good work he had started and knowing I could leave the results to him.

There have been times when I've prayed for someone and seen an instant healing; other times the healing comes more gradually; and sometimes the healing is invisible as it's more of an emotional or spiritual healing. I don't try to figure any of that out. That's not my job; my job is to ask for healing, and it's God's job to be God.

When God leads me to pray for someone, I first ask that person if it's okay to pray. Once I gain their permission, I tell my friend,

"I'm going to pray for you because I know God hears our prayers, and I'm going to pray in joy because I know how much God loves you. I don't know exactly how God will answer my prayer, but I know that he is able to do more than I ask.

So, I'm going to pray, trusting that he will answer with his love."

What a pleasure to pray for others this way. Try it! Don't hold back because you're afraid you'll be disappointed—because if you don't pray, your disappointment will be certain.

> The best thing about praying with joy is that joy brings faith and faith brings miracles.

As for Renee, my young assistant (whom I mentioned in chapter 3), and her battle with cancer, as we prayed, God healed her through a series of chemo treatments. But the exciting news is, she only needed half the treatments originally planned. As far as I'm concerned, I'm thanking God; we got our miracle.

The Healing Secret

Not long ago I heard from an old college friend who told me he'd lost his faith. "What I don't get," Terry said, "is if God is God, why don't amputees' limbs grow back?"

Later, I mentioned Terry's question in front of my daughter. Knowing she might not understand what the word *amputee* meant, I explained it by telling her that an amputee was someone who could not use their arms or legs. To my surprise, Laura began to laugh in a way I've rarely seen. Great and loud guffaws filled the air, and tears ran down her cheeks.

"What is so funny?" I asked.

Poor Laura couldn't catch her breath, and her hoots wouldn't stop. It took a while before she was calm enough to communicate with me.

"Laura, is that funny because when you were in heaven, you saw people with new arms and legs?"

"Yes!" Laura told me through her tongue signals as another peal of laughter started.

Then it hit me, and I asked my paralyzed daughter, "Laura, were you one of those people?"

"Yes! Yes!" she signaled again.

When I later told Terry how my disabled daughter had responded to his stumbling block, Terry came back to Christ.

It all goes to show that our understanding of healing is limited. So keep hoping, keep praying, keep asking with joy, because God hears you and is moving on your behalf.

Visit www.IgniteMyFaith.com, Chapter Videos, then Chapter 10, to see me tell this story, as well as video clips of my precious daughter laughing.

Trip to the Oasis

Pray this worshipful prayer of David as he praised God for healing and forgiveness of sins.

> Praise the LORD, my soul;
>> all my inmost being, praise his holy name.
> Praise the LORD, my soul,
>> and forget not all his benefits—
> who forgives all your sins
>> and heals all your diseases,
> who redeems your life from the pit
>> and crowns you with love and compassion,
> who satisfies your desires with good things
>> so that your youth is renewed like the eagle's.
> The LORD works righteousness

and justice for all the oppressed.
He made known his ways to Moses,
his deeds to the people of Israel:
The LORD is compassionate and gracious,
slow to anger, abounding in love.
He will not always accuse,
nor will he harbor his anger forever;
he does not treat us as our sins deserve
or repay us according to our iniquities.
For as high as the heavens are above
the earth,
so great is his love for those who
fear him;
as far as the east is from the west,
so far has he removed our trans-
gressions from us.
As a father has compassion on
his children,
so the LORD has compassion on
those who fear him;
for he knows how we are formed,
he remembers that we are dust.
The life of mortals is like grass,
they flourish like a flower of the field;
the wind blows over it and it is gone,
and its place remembers it no more.
But from everlasting to everlasting
the LORD's love is with those who fear him,
and his righteousness with their children's children—
with those who keep his covenant
and remember to obey his precepts. (Ps. 103:1–18)

> Don't hold back because you're afraid you'll be disappointed—because if you don't pray, your disappointment will be certain.

PRAYER EXPERIENCE

Dear Lord,

I ask for your strength to hope, to believe, and to trust you with all that is going on in my life and the lives of my loved ones. Erase my doubts and fill me with confidence in you.

I ask that you would give me the gift of praying the prayer of faith as you heal me and my loved ones. Thank you for the gift of your miracles.

In the name of Jesus,

Amen

11

The Peace That Passes Understanding

God cannot give us a happiness and peace apart from Himself,
because it is not there. There is no such thing.

—C. S. Lewis[1]

It was 12:30 p.m., May 22, 2008, and there wasn't a cloud in the sky.
I was fast approaching the Dacono exit on I-25 in my Ford Taurus
wagon, running late to host the afternoon taping of the *Denver*
Celebration TV show. As I drove, I listened to praise music on the
radio and thought about the three minute monologue I would give
to open the program. I asked the Lord, "Is there anything you'd
like me to say?"

I felt, or rather heard, his still small voice in my inner ear: "I am
with you to give you peace in the storm."

As I began to think how wonderful it was that God provides
peace in the storms of life, a shiny cloud blotted out the road ahead.
Where did that *come from?* I wondered, sure it hadn't been there

a second ago. I glanced at the oil tanker in the lane next to me. I felt nervous to enter this storm with the tanker so near. So I hit the gas and tried to pull ahead. I guess the tanker's driver had the same idea, and so we hit the cloud together, going about eighty miles an hour. I was shocked by the loud *crack!* that shuddered through my car as it hit the cloud. Not only did the road in front of me disappear, but so did the tanker beside me. The wind and water were so overpowering that I could see nothing beyond the inside of my windshield, which I feared would shatter into pieces.

Lord, I'm glad you're with me in this storm, I prayed as I tried to hold the steering wheel steady, hoping I could stay in my lane— *wherever* it was. Suddenly, the tanker and my Taurus broke through the wall of wind and water and entered into a wide open space filled with softly swirling fog.

What a strange storm cell, I thought as I turned up the praise music. *But you're right, God; there* is *peace in the storm!*

As my heart worshiped along with the song on the radio, I noted that cars were huddled beneath the overpass a couple of hundred yards ahead. *Why are they afraid of a little fog?* I wondered.

After I passed them, I saw another wall. This one didn't seem as thick as the first wall, and I could even see daylight shining through it. The driver of the oil tanker and I didn't hold back. We hit that wall, drove through the wind and into the sunshine. Minutes later, the radio beeped an emergency alert and the computer-generated voice said, "There is a tornado on I-25 at the Dacono exit."[2]

Say what?

Sure enough, my oil tanker friend and I had just driven through one of the twelve tornadoes that touched down around Colorado that day. I hadn't recognized the storm as a tornado because it wasn't shaped like a cone. It was in fact a half-mile-wide wedge tornado. Who knew tornadoes came in different shapes?

But the real question is how could I, as well as that tanker, have driven right through the heart of a large tornado?

The answer can only be that God was with us to give us peace in the storm.

And no matter what you're going through, know this: God is with you to give you peace in your storm.

Finding Peace in Your Storm

I'd like to call your attention back to when Peter walked on the water with Jesus. Imagine the moments before the miracle when Peter and the disciples huddled in their small boat against the sudden squall. With Jesus back on shore, the men had to battle the wind and the waves alone.

But as it turned out, they *weren't* alone because Jesus was all the while coming to their rescue. When Peter saw Jesus walking across the water, he climbed out of the boat and ran across the tops of the waves to Jesus. The moment his focus shifted from Jesus to the waves, he sank beneath them. But Peter rose above his circumstances by shifting his focus back to Jesus with his cry, "Lord, save me!" (Matt. 14:30).

> No matter what you're going through, know this: God is with you to give you peace in your storm.

Sometimes, you may find yourself, like Peter, battered by the storms of life. The first thing you need to do when a storm hits is to look for Jesus. When you see him, run to him. Never mind the gusts of wind or swelling problems, *run*. And if waves of troubles trip you, call out to the name above every name, "Lord, save me!"

When you make that call, miracles happen and what seemed impossible before will become a reality.

I met a woman at the Colorado Christian Writer's Conference who told me that due to a flat tire, her family had pulled their car out of the line of cars waiting for the ferry and headed back home to spend the night, determined to escape Crystal Beach, Texas, first thing the next morning. But Hurricane Ike made an early arrival, trapping the family in the rising storm surge that swept in not only from the beach in front of their home but also from the inlet behind them. They watched from their porch as the two storm surges crashed together in violent waves, making it impossible to run toward the rescue chopper that hovered nearby. The chopper couldn't land in the colliding waves, and it appeared the family would die in a watery grave. That's when my friend's little daughter led the family in prayer, asking God to part the waters just as he parted the Red Sea. And to everyone's amazement, the waters parted, and the helicopter landed and rescued the family before the hurricane's surge swept their home off the face of the earth.

Their cry of "Lord, save me!" was answered in a way that once again calmed the storm.

Invite God's Presence into the Storm

When the Lord reached out to Peter bobbing in the waves, Peter was able to rise and walk. Matthew 14:32–33 continues the story, "And when they climbed into the boat, the wind died down. Then those who were in the boat worshiped him, saying, 'Truly you are the Son of God.'"

Just like the disciples invited Jesus into their boat, we can invite the presence of the Lord into our troubles. Our lives will not capsize because the presence of Jesus brings peace.

Kay Arthur said, "Where do *you* run when you need peace? Is your first response to go looking for a person or to pick up the phone? Before you do, Beloved, run into the shelter of His name. When you find Him, you will find peace because . . . He *is* peace."[3]

The awesome thing about being a follower of Christ is that at the moment we give our lives to God and ask him to forgive us of our sins through the work of Jesus on the cross, his Holy Spirit comes to dwell inside of us. Jesus said, "And I will ask the Father, and he will give you another advocate to help you and be with you forever—the Spirit of truth. The world cannot accept him, because it neither sees him nor knows him. But you know him, for he lives with you and will be in you" (John 14:16–17).

> Just like the disciples invited Jesus into their boat, we can invite the presence of the Lord into our troubles. Our lives will not capsize because the presence of Jesus brings peace.

Paul said in Ephesians 1:17–18, "I keep asking that the God of our Lord Jesus Christ, the glorious Father, may give you the Spirit of wisdom and revelation, so that you may know him better."

We need to know him better, to understand that we can abide with him and have more of his presence within us, as Jesus said in Luke 17:21: "The kingdom of God is within you" (NKJV).

Once you discover that though you are *not* God, his presence is *in* you through Jesus, you begin to recognize his presence and ask for more.

Andrew Murray, in his book *Absolute Surrender*, gives four simple steps on how to be filled with more of God's Holy Spirit. First, he tells us to say, "I *must* be filled."[4]

Murray encourages, "Say it to God from the depths of your heart. 'God commands it; I cannot live my life as I should without it.'"[5]

Second, Murray teaches us to say, "I *may* be filled. It is possible; the promise is for me."[6]

Murray explains, "The apostles, once so full of pride and self-life, were filled with the Holy Spirit because they took hold of

Jesus. Likewise, with all your own pride, sin, and self, if you will but cling to Him, you may be filled."[7]

Third, Murray encourages us to say, "I *would* be filled."[8]

Murray believed, "To gain the 'pearl of great price' you must sell all, give up everything. You are willing, are you not? 'Everything, Lord, if I may only have your Spirit. Lord, I would have it from you now.'"[9]

Finally, Murray recommends we say, "I *shall* be filled. God longs to give it; I shall have it."[10]

Murray says,

> Never mind whether it comes as a flood or in deep silence; or whether it does not come now because God is preparing you for it tomorrow. But say, "*I shall be filled*. If I entrust myself to Jesus, He will not disappoint me." It is His very nature, it is His work in heaven, and it is His delight to give His people the Holy Spirit in full measure. Claim it now: "My God, it is such a serious thing; it is awesome, almost too blessed to be true—Lord, will you not do it? My trembling heart says, *I shall be filled with the Holy Spirit*."[11]

Reread Murray's four statements as a prayer and open your heart for more of the Holy Spirit in your life.

Have Faith That God Is with You

The Lord is with you in your boat. Like Peter, learn to recognize him and call to him, and know that he will never let you go it alone. You may fail him; you may make mistakes that make you think he's tossed you aside, but know that he loves you with an everlasting love. He forgives you the moment you ask. So, if you feel separated from him, pray this:

Dear Lord,

Sometimes the storm drowns out my ability to feel your presence; sometimes the sins of fear and doubt and other problems creep in to steal my confidence in you and your love for me. So Lord, I ask you to give me the faith to know that your presence, your Holy Spirit, is with me. Forgive me for my fear and doubt and give me your confidence and assurance to make it through the storm.

In Jesus' name,
Amen

How Do You Find Peace If You Yourself Caused the Storm?

Recently I was doing a radio interview and the talk show host asked, "But Linda, what do you do if you are the cause of the storm in your life?"

That's a great question. If you are the one, willfully or even unwittingly, that caused your problems, does that mean God will look down at you from his heavenly throne and shake his head as if to say, "Well, you got what you deserved now, didn't you!"

If you are a true believer, God will never leave you or your circumstances unless you

> You may fail him; you may make mistakes that make you think he's tossed you aside, but know that he loves you with an everlasting love. He forgives you the moment you ask.

1. kick him out
2. leave him out
3. ignore him

So, let's say you *have* created your own problems. (And who among us hasn't done things that adversely affected our lives or the lives of others?) Is there a remedy?

Yes! Invite God back into your situation. Jesus says in Revelation 3:20, "Here I am! I stand at the door and knock. If anyone hears my voice and opens the door, I will come in and eat with that person, and they with me."

Jesus is asking permission to come into every area of your life, including your troubles. And if you are the one who caused the trouble, the presence of Jesus can still make all the difference.

In fact, I believe too many people live in deep regret, secretly wanting to punish themselves for poor choices or actions even more than wanting God to turn their situation into a miracle. But again, Romans 8:28 says, "And we know that in all things God works for the good of those who love him, who have been called according to his purpose." This even applies to circumstances where choices go wrong. Pray this:

Dear Lord,

I've made a mistake(s) I deeply regret and I take responsibility for the pain and chaos my mistake(s) caused. Please forgive me. I invite you into my troubles and lay my mistake(s) down at the foot of the cross. Please turn my mistake(s) into a miracle.

In the name of Jesus,
Amen

Yes, you might have to live with the consequences of your mistakes, but with God, it's going to be all right. Lamentations says, "The faithful love of the LORD never ends! His mercies never cease. Great is his faithfulness; his mercies begin afresh each morning" (3:22–23 NLT). And it really is true. Jesus paid it all.

Once, I met a woman through GodTest.com who had embezzled thousands from her employer. Her boyfriend abandoned her when she was caught, convicted, and sentenced to jail. Stacey was beside herself with grief and decided that the only solution was to take her own life. She emailed me to say she had a "plan" and that she was saying good-bye because she could not live with her consequences.

"Stacey, don't kill yourself!" I encouraged. "Let's invite God into your situation and ask that he turn it into a miracle."

So instead of committing suicide that night, this dear lady prayed with me. However, though her prayer kept her alive, it did not keep her out of prison. She served her time, and when she got out, she wrote me to say, "Thank you for talking me out of

> Yes, you might have to live with the consequences of your mistakes, but with God, it's going to be all right.

suicide. I survived jail and now have a new job. I've met someone who has become the love of my life. I'm writing to share my joy and to tell you that I'm getting married."

Wow, Stacey served her time and now has a brand new life because she let God have a place in her circumstance caused by her own mistakes. When she invited God's presence in, God turned her very life into a miracle. A new day has dawned in Stacey's life, fresh with the everlasting mercies and grace of God.

Peace Be Still

The time Peter walked across the water with Jesus is not the only time Jesus stilled the storm. Let's read Mark 4:37–41, when Jesus, after a long day of preaching, got in a boat with his disciples to cross the Sea of Galilee.

> A furious squall came up, and the waves broke over the boat, so that it was nearly swamped. Jesus was in the stern, sleeping on a cushion. The disciples woke him and said to him, "Teacher, don't you care if we drown?"

He got up, rebuked the wind and said to the waves, "Quiet! Be still!" Then the wind died down and it was completely calm.

He said to his disciples, "Why are you so afraid? Do you still have no faith?"

They were terrified and asked each other, "Who is this? Even the wind and the waves obey him!"

Perhaps you sometimes feel like the disciples when they found that Jesus was asleep in the middle of their crisis. Have you ever called out to the Lord but found him to be unresponsive?

When the Lord is silent, that does not mean he's not present. As long as you're in his boat, you are safe. Just as Peter couldn't sink when he focused on Jesus, the disciples' boat couldn't sink when the presence of Jesus rested inside of it, storm or no storm.

> **When the Lord is silent, that does not mean he's not present. As long as he's in your boat, you are safe.**

Last winter, I spent a couple of days at a church in Parker, Colorado, speaking at their women's conference. But before I left for the event, I called the meeting planner. "Looks like that big blizzard is scheduled to hit tonight," I told her. "Are you going ahead with the conference, or do you think you might cancel?"

"We're praying that God will put a bubble around us, and we're moving ahead," Wanda told me. And to my surprise, despite the forecast, the church was filled with women. But the funny thing was that though the blizzard hit this area of Colorado hard, the church property itself remained practically snow free.

The next morning, the snow-free blizzard continued. The winds howled and the vent in the auditorium rattled as if competing with my talk.

As I led the women in a moment of silence, I said, "Now, let's be still before God."

The vent continued its rattle, and I looked up and pointed and said, "And that means you too."

In that instant, the vent stopped rattling. It remained silent until we said, "Amen."

It was a case of "Quiet! Be still!" The cool thing is, through Jesus, we have the power to say, "Quiet! Be still!" through any storm we may face.

Running from God

Perhaps you, like Jonah, have refused to obey God. When God asked Jonah to carry the message of repentance to the town of Nineveh, Jonah refused and boarded a boat headed in the opposite direction. That's when God used a storm to put Jonah back in his place. When the sailors realized the storm was sent for Jonah, they threw him overboard, where he was promptly swallowed by a whale. Jonah called to the Lord from the belly of the whale, saying, "When my life was ebbing away, I remembered you, LORD, and my prayer rose to you, to your holy temple" (Jon. 2:7).

> Your storms will not last forever, but you can seek and find the peace of God to carry you through.

God heard Jonah and caused the whale to vomit Jonah onto the shore. Soon, Jonah was back on his way to Nineveh. There he completed his original assignment and preached repentance to a receptive people.

If you, like Jonah, are on the run from God and you find yourself caught in a storm, perhaps you need to do what Jonah did and go back to obey God. When you do, you will find peace.

Last spring, I stood in front of a camera while filming my internet TV show, *True Miracles*, as a sheet of rain poured behind me. I said to the camera, "The storms of life will not last forever, one day the rain *will* stop."

As if on cue, the pouring rain slowed to a dribble, the sky brightened, and the birds took to song. I believe God provided these special effects to help me make my point. Your storms will not last forever, but you can seek and find the peace of God to carry you through.[12]

Trip to the Oasis

Pray this paraphrased prayer of David as he talks to the God of storms and of peace:

> Lord, we, your mighty ones, say you are the Lord of glory
> and strength.
> Glory is due your name and we worship you in the splendor of your holiness.
> Your voice is over the waters.
> Your voice, O Lord, strikes with flashes of lightning.
> Your voice shakes the desert and twists the oaks and strips the forests bare.
> And all in your temple cry, "Glory!"
> You, O Lord, sit enthroned over the flood;
> you are enthroned as King forever.
> You, O Lord, give strength to your people;
> you bless your people with peace. (Ps. 29:1–4, 7–11)

PRAYER EXPERIENCE

Dear Lord,

Please bless me with peace, even when I walk through the storms of rejection, betrayal, lack, strife, or trouble. For as I have invited you to join me, I know you are with me in the storm. Forgive me if I have traveled away from you or your purposes; help me to return to and obey you. As I walk with you through the storm, I say in the name of Jesus, "Quiet! Be still!"

In Jesus' name,

Amen

To continue in prayer with me, go to www.IgniteMyFaith.com, Chapter Videos, Chapter 11.

12

Find Real Joy

Perhaps God brings us to the end of our resources so we can discover the vastness of His.

—Neil T. Anderson[1]

We walk this earth for one purpose: to worship, trust, and seek the Lord. But can he be found? Yes, as you recall from the first chapter, the directions to find God consist of a seeking heart, for as Jeremiah 29:13 says, "You will seek me and find me when you seek me with all your heart."

When our heart cries for God, we *will* find him. But we must truly seek *him* and not just the answers to our prayer requests. This means that we must be willing to trust him when his plans aren't our plans. Otherwise, we'll be like the preschooler who prayed, "Thank you for the baby brother, God, but what I prayed for was a puppy."

When we seek favors from God over seeking God himself, we may find ourselves in a battle with God's will. Peter fought God's will by actually arguing with Jesus himself, as we read in Mark 8.

> He [Jesus] then began to teach them [the disciples] that the Son of Man must suffer many things and be rejected by the elders, the chief priests and the teachers of the law, and that he must be killed and after three days rise again. He spoke plainly about this, and Peter took him aside and began to rebuke him.
>
> But when Jesus turned and looked at his disciples, he rebuked Peter. "Get behind me, Satan!" he said. "You do not have in mind the things of God, but merely human concerns." (vv. 31–33)

Even after this rebuke, Peter continued to fight God's will. When the soldiers and their entourage came to arrest Jesus, Peter pulled out his sword and cut off a man's ear. Jesus responded by healing the man and then allowing the soldiers to arrest him, a step he had to take to complete his destiny.

But Peter didn't understand. He fought God's will because the situation seemed unthinkable. Perhaps you too are experiencing the unthinkable. Perhaps you are like me more than twenty years ago, when I kept insisting that God completely heal my injured daughter. When God didn't move the way I asked, I wondered how I'd failed to convince him. I mean, how could God use such a terrible circumstance for good? I didn't believe it was possible.

Now, when I look back on my quest to move God, I can see what I couldn't see then. God *had* heard me and was moving to turn my circumstances for good. I can say this because my disabled daughter has lived her life to his glory. As I think of the people she's touched along the way, the people who would have never come to Christ without her precious spirit and testimony, I rejoice. I think of Laura's young friend, Jessica Hunter, who died in a terrible car crash on I-25. As Jessica's mother told me, Jessica is in heaven today in part because of Laura's influence on her life. Laura helped Jess develop compassion, and compassion became an influence that helped direct Jessica to the Lord. What a blessing it was for Jessica's mother to know that her sixteen-year-old daughter's sudden departure meant her sudden arrival to be with Jesus.

Twenty years ago, when I pleaded for God to answer my prayers on my daughter's behalf, I couldn't have known God's will didn't *exactly* match my prayers. But with time, I learned to trust God even though I didn't understand his ways.

We all need help in seeking God and his will. Even David prayed, "Teach me to do your will" (Ps. 143:10). Jesus himself prayed, "Your kingdom come, your will be done, on earth as it is in heaven" (Matt. 6:10).

I am telling you this, not because I don't believe God is going to answer your prayers. I *know* God will turn your requests into miracles. I *know* he is with you and will help you rise above your circumstances. But I also know you can find contentment along your journey no matter what you

> You're going to get a miracle whether he changes your circumstances or changes you.

are going through—for as Paul said in Philippians, "For I have learned to be content whatever the circumstances. I know what it is to be in need, and I know what it is to have plenty. I have learned the secret of being content in any and every situation, whether well fed or hungry, whether living in plenty or in want. I can do all this through him who gives me strength" (4:11–13).

You may still be wondering, hey, it's great that God can give me strength, but does God have the power to change my circumstances?

Of course he does. You're going to get a miracle whether he changes your circumstances or he changes you. The key is to seek God's face with your whole heart. For the Lord says, "'I will be found by you,' declares the Lord, 'and will bring you back from captivity'" (Jer. 29:14).

Shepherd's Hierarchy of Faith

To seek God's face, you must go deeper in your personal relationship with him. To help, I've created what I call "Shepherd's Hierarchy of Faith," which includes the following levels of faith:

1. **Need**—recognizing our need for God.
2. **Hear**—hearing and understanding the why of Christ's crucifixion and resurrection.
3. **Faith**—calling on or believing in the name of Jesus.
4. **Transform**—experiencing God's transforming power to be forgiven, to forgive others, and to release your burdens to him. (In other words, to be transformed by God instead of conformed to this world.)
5. **Holy Spirit**—encouraging the presence of the Holy Spirit.
6. **Lordship**—learning how to trust God with our circumstances and our very lives.
7. **Abiding Presence**—abiding in the Christ in us, who is also in heavenly places.

I'm not sure where you started when you opened this book, but I'm hoping you are finding your way to level seven and are learning to abide in Christ's presence.

When we abide with Christ:

- we experience his love
- we rest in him
- we obey him
- we thank and worship him

We Experience His Love

Paul, in Ephesians 3:16–19, prayed that we would be strengthened in the power of his spirit and that we would have the power to truly grasp God's love for us, so that we would be filled with God's presence.

It's hard to grasp how much God loves us and longs for our time, attention, and focus—especially when we seem to be preoccupied with everything but building our friendship with him. For even while we're busy learning *about* God, we often forget to spend time getting to *know* him. When we do come to him to ask a request or two, we forget that he wants to use our time together to build a deeper relationship.

It's kind of like the time my son Jim was a toddler and we were shopping at the mall. When I suddenly realized it was way past his bedtime, I hurried Jimmy through Sears in a mad dash to the parking lot. That's when Jimmy suddenly flopped to the white-tiled floor. "I'm tired," he said, grabbing my snow boot in an arm lock. "Could you drag me for a while?"

I leaned over him. "I don't think I can drag you, but I can carry you. Would that be okay?"

Jimmy looked up and nodded, and I scooped him into my arms. His blue eyes closed as he instantly fell asleep next to my heart.

What happened between my son and me also happens in our relationship with God. We get so focused on our prayer requests that we forget he longs to have a deeper relationship with us. It's like we throw ourselves at his feet and plead, "God, I know you don't want to bother with me right now because you're busy with a million more important things, but I don't think I can go on. Could you just drag me for a while?"

But just as I didn't want to drag my son down a dusty floor and into the parking lot, God doesn't want to drag us through the muck of this world. He wants to lovingly scoop us into his everlasting arms and carry us through our difficulties. We can rest in him as he carries us through. As Deuteronomy 33:27 says, "The eternal God is your refuge, and underneath are the everlasting arms."

So let's duly note that it's impossible to abide with Christ without experiencing his great love. For when we abide with him, our eyes are opened and we experience more of his love than we ever thought possible. Rick Warren put it this way: "God is love. He didn't need us. But he wanted us. And that is the most amazing thing."[2]

Jesus speaks of this great love when he said, "As the Father loved Me, I also have loved you; abide in My love. If you keep My commandments, you will abide in My love, just as I have kept My Father's commandments and abide in His love" (John 15:9–10 NKJV).

But the funny thing is, as we abide in his love, our hearts open to love others. John said in 1 John, "If we love one another, God abides in us, and His love has been perfected in us. By this we know that we abide in Him, and He in us, because He has given us of His Spirit" (4:12–13 NKJV).

We Rest in Him

God longs for us to rest in him. But it's impossible to rest when we're busy worrying through our difficulties. I'm usually pretty good at trusting God, but not so much this past week. I had a tough ministry decision to make that had unthinkable consequences if I should make the wrong choice. How important it was that I hear God's voice and follow his lead! So I spent the week praying and fasting and rebuking the enemy. I spent sleepless nights weeping into my pillow and always, always straining to hear God's voice.

By Friday, I was exhausted and I still wasn't sure what direction God wanted me to take. The only thing I'd been able to hear from him was, "Rejoice! I am with you. Everything is going to be okay."

But I was so focused on hearing my answer that I missed the breakthrough: *God is with me. Everything is going to be all right!*

I had my promise, yet I didn't rest in him. I chose to spend my time fretting when I could have spent my week rejoicing. Now, I'm not saying it was wrong for me to seek God, but when I heard from him, I missed the opportunity to rejoice and rest in him. And sure enough, God came through with the direction I needed just in the nick of time. So, all that stress was for nothing. (Oh, forgive me, Lord!)

But what God promised me, he's already promised you. When you seek him, know that he is with you. Know he is guiding you. As you learn to trust him, you'll see that everything is going to be all right. He's going to complete the good work he has already begun in you, and you will have your answers in the nick of time. So, what are you waiting for? Rest and rejoice!

> When you seek him, know that he is with you. Know he is guiding you. As you learn to trust him, you'll see that everything is going to be all right.

We Obey Him

One day my office phone rang. When I glanced at the caller ID, it read, "Christ the King."

What?! I gulped and determined that no matter the question asked, my response would be, "Yes!"

The caller identified herself. "Hi, Linda, this is Ruby calling from Christ the King Presbyterian Church in Castle Rock. I was wondering if you would come and speak to our ladies."

I grinned and answered, "Of course! How could I say no to Christ the King?"

Sometimes God's direction is clear and all we have to do is follow him. But sometimes God's direction is hard to find. Carole, my prayer partner, once fought the good fight in a prayer concern, but her prayer request was answered with a no.

Though Carole was troubled by God's answer, she felt led to praise God anyway. As she did, God's still small voice spoke to her, "I know you were disappointed in the answer to your prayer, but you were obedient to praise me."

Carole was obedient to him because she completely surrendered to him. Sometimes God wants us to put aside our disappointments and completely surrender to him in praise, signifying our trust in him.

Margaret Feinberg explains it like this:

> True surrender is not a single action but a posture in life, yielding ourselves—our whole selves—to God. Breathtaking opportunities for surrender will surface throughout our lives, but grabbing hold of them begins below the surface, in the deep places of the soul where God is already preparing us not just for those moments but for himself.[3]

We Thank and Worship Him

To be completed in God may have nothing to do with getting your prayers answered the way you want; to be completed in God is more about worshiping him. When Jesus healed the ten lepers, only one received a greater miracle when he fell at Jesus' feet and worshiped. He alone received the higher revelation of Christ.

If you are reading this book because you are seeking relief from your pain and circumstances, you will find relief not by getting your prayer requests answered the way you hope but by falling on your face and worshiping God despite your circumstances. For when you worship God, his very presence will abide with you.

About six hundred years before Christ was born of a virgin, the land of Babylon had a great king named Nebuchadnezzar. Nebuchadnezzar commissioned a ninety-foot-tall image of gold and commanded all in the land to worship it. However, Shadrach, Meshach, and Abednego refused to bow down because they only worshiped God Almighty. But when the king learned of their insubordination, he threatened to burn them alive in his furnace.

But Shadrach, Meshach, and Abednego refused to worship Nebuchadnezzar's false god. They told the king that even if they were tossed into the fire, the God they served would be able to save them. They said, "But even if he does not, we want you to know, Your Majesty, that we will not serve your gods or worship the image of gold you have set up" (Dan. 3:18).

> You will find relief not by getting your prayer requests answered the way you hope but by falling on your face and worshiping God despite your circumstances. For when you worship God, his very presence will abide with you.

Nebuchadnezzar was so furious that he turned his furnace setting to "roast," then had his strongest soldiers toss his three captives into the fire. Even before the soldiers could step back from the blaze they were overcome by the heat and died.

As the king watched the furnace, instead of seeing his prisoners burn, he saw they stood alongside a fourth man. Nebuchadnezzar said, "Look! I see four men walking around in the fire, unbound and unharmed, and the fourth looks like a son of the gods."

Nebuchadnezzar then approached the opening of the blazing furnace and shouted, "Shadrach, Meshach, and Abednego, servants of the Most High God, come out! Come here!"

So Shadrach, Meshach, and Abednego came out of the fire, and the satraps, prefects, governors, and royal advisers crowded around them. They saw that the fire had not harmed their bodies, nor was a hair of their heads singed; their robes were not scorched, and there was no smell of fire on them (Dan. 3:25–27).

> No matter what kind of fire we find ourselves in, the presence of God will protect us as we worship him and him alone.

Shadrach, Meshach, and Abednego were not consumed by the problem of being tossed into a fiery furnace because the presence of God was with them! And the same is true of us. No matter what kind of fire we find ourselves in, the presence of God will protect us as we worship him and him alone. So worship him, not for what you can get him to do for you but because you want to thank him for his presence; because you want to thank him for the many blessings he has already given you; because you want to thank him that you don't have to carry your burdens; and because you want to thank him for his great love for you.

Worship the one who made you to rejoice in him, who gives you his joy as your strength. As you worship, you'll discover that your troubles are only the seeds of miracles that God is planting throughout your life.

First Thessalonians 5:16–18 says, "Rejoice always, pray continually, give thanks in all circumstances; for this is God's will for you in Christ Jesus."

Could it be that God allows difficulties so we can learn how to pray without ceasing, and thus stay in relationship with him as we learn how to rejoice always?

Then this is good news because despite what you are going through, you can rest your troubled heart in the presence of God. As you allow your troubles to teach you how to abide in Christ, you will reach level seven of Shepherd's Hierarchy of Faith as you surrender your hindrances of

- bitterness and pain
- jealousy and envy
- anger and strife
- discontentment
- worry and fear
- disappointment and grief

You will know you are learning to abide with him when you yourself stop being the hindrance to more of God's presence in your life. For the truth is, when you remove your hindrances, you can have as much of God as you want.

Choose his presence over worry; choose his joy even in your pain; and choose his will over your own. Recognize your need for him, reflect on what he's done for you, call on his name, transform your life in his power, open your life to more of his Holy Spirit, trust him with every aspect of your life, and abide with him. In so doing, experience his love for you, rest in him, obey him, and give thanks as you worship him.

Above all, seek God first. As you do, you will experience the miracle of his presence in the fiery furnace, and you will find real joy.

Trip to the Oasis

Pray my joyful, paraphrased psalm of King David:

> I will shout for joy to the Lord, all the earth.
> I will worship the Lord with gladness;

I will come before him with joyful songs.

For I know that the Lord is God.

He made me, I am his;

I am a lamb in his pasture.

I will enter his gates with thanksgiving

and his courts with praise;

I will give thanks to him and praise his name.

For the Lord is good and his love endures forever;

his faithfulness continues through all generations.

(100:1–5)

Prayer Experience

Dear Lord,

I do not want to be the hindrance to your presence in my life and circumstances, so help me to step out of the way. By an act of my will, I ask for your supernatural power to help me release my bitterness and pain, jealousy and envy, anger and strife, discontentment, worry and fear and disappointment—to you.

Help me to abide with you. I choose your presence over worry, your joy over pain, your will over my own. I thank you and bless your holy name. I confess that I need you. I thank you for Jesus' completed work on the cross and resurrection from the dead. I call on the gift of Jesus for the forgiveness of my sins so that I can walk with you. I ask that you transform me as you help me to forgive. I ask that you transform me as I lay my burdens at the foot of the cross. I invite your Holy Spirit into my life. I trust you with every aspect of my life as I abide with you. Lord, help me to know and relax in your great love for me. Give me the supernatural ability to trust you and rest in you. Give me the strength to obey you. I give thanks in all my circumstances and worship you and you alone. I seek you first. Give me your joy as my strength as I praise your holy name. Be with me in the fire. Lord, may your presence change everything.

In Jesus' name,

Amen

Listen to me discuss how to count your blessings in www .IgniteMyFaith.com, Chapter Videos, then Chapter 12.

Bible Study and Discussion Guide

Five minutes after I finished the first draft of this book, a full-blown crisis hit me with such force that I could hardly breathe. But a few days later, I was stunned to find that as I edited this manuscript, it read as a letter straight from God to me. My perspective of my crisis was transformed with hope. What comfort I found as I continued to review these tried-and-true principles that have helped me not only survive my difficulties but thrive despite them.

With the storm still swirling about me, I have the peace that passes understanding. I am able to walk with the Lord, and in so doing, I've found a place to rest in him and to find real joy. For I recognize that this crisis is an open door to breakthrough. I can only thank God for this miracle, just as you can thank God that he is also moving in your circumstances. For like Peter, we are in the same boat, and the only solution is to step into the storm and run to Jesus. When we keep our focus on him, we will not slip into the waves but will walk across them as we hold on tight to him. So hold on! Everything is going to work out for the good.

Dear friends, I hope this book gives the hope and focus you need to rise above your troubles. Now I pray that it will also bring you deeper fellowship as you answer and discuss the following questions, which were written with group discussions in mind; however, feel free to adapt them for your own personal use. Also note that there is a short video that goes with each chapter. View the videos at www.IgniteMyFaith.com, then click on Chapter Videos.

With love,

Linda

Chapter 1: When Difficulties Come

1. List three to five reasons why we shouldn't give up on God.
2. Describe the sufferings of Jesus and explain the reasons he chose to endure his sufferings.
3. Read James 1:2–3 and explain why we should choose joy. Can you think of a time you chose joy in a difficulty? Share it.
4. Think of Moses's life as well as your own, then explain how God can use a desert detour to make you a better person.
5. Read the entire 43rd Psalm, then discuss reasons and ways to find hope in the desert times of life.
6. Is it possible to put one's hope in God during a crisis? How? Discuss as many ways and ideas as you can.
7. Read the prayer at the end of chapter 1 aloud.

Chapter 2: Finding God in Your Circumstances

1. Read Jeremiah 29:13 and discuss how it is a guide to direct you to God.
2. Is happiness really a choice? Isn't it really based on our circumstances? Please describe good that came out of a difficulty you experienced. Compare your blessings with Linda's list of blessings that came out of her difficulty.

3. What was the miracle Linda found when she clung to God? Create a prayer to help you turn to God in a difficulty.

4. Think of a trauma you've experienced then re-pray the trauma prayer to help you find relief from your trauma.

5. How does one abide with God? Read aloud the prayer example given in the chapter to help you abide with God.

6. Read 1 Corinthians 3:16 then discuss why this truth is the first step to abiding with God.

7. Jesus seemed moved by Mary's grief at the death of her brother Lazarus. Why did she weep when Jesus was about to raise Lazarus from the dead? How does this story apply to us?

8. Discuss Anne Graham Lotz's gift and how and why she tossed it in the trash. How does this story apply to how we see God and the treasures he has put in our lives?

9. Read Psalm 3 and share your thoughts on how God is the God of deliverance.

Chapter 3: Five Keys to Surviving Difficult Times

1. Take turns reading the nine listed reasons as to why tragedy happens. Identify the reason that struck you as most interesting and explain why.

2. What should our response to suffering be? What can you do to help someone who is suffering? Discuss that plan.

3. Why did King David need God to help him create a clean heart? Why do we?

4. Tell one to three reasons why you can thank God in your current circumstances.

5. How can our perception of our circumstances fail us? What are some ways to tap into God's perspective?

6. What did you learn from Linda's story about "bat practice"? How does this story apply to you?

7. Reread and discuss Andrew Murray's quote about prayer. Why do you agree or disagree with his conclusion?

8. Read Psalm 51 out loud, together, as a prayer. Describe how this exercise meant to you.

Chapter 4: Giving Your Troubles to God

1. Read Matthew 11:28–30, then 1 Peter 5:7. Discuss how the women from both Iowa and Nebraska were set free. How can you?

2. How does Linda's suitcases-in-the-subway story compare to our personal lives? Pray the prayer example aloud to give God your burdens.

3. Why were Mika and David angry at God? Tell about a time you felt that way. What's the solution to our envy of the wicked?

4. Read the list of blessings that David mentions, then call out your favorite blessing on the list.

5. What did the Lord say to comfort Moses when he was worried about leading the Israelites? How do those words apply to you?

6. How did the meaning of Noah's name speak to his purpose? How does this word speak to your purpose? Pray the prayer of rest out loud.

7. Reread Psalm 27. Explain how the end of the passage speaks to you personally.

8. Read the prayer experience aloud. Explain how this prayer has helped or applies to you.

Chapter 5: Standing Against the Darkness

1. Name some ways that a person can come under the influence of the evil one.

2. Read John 10:10. Why does the enemy come against us?

3. Read 1 John 4:4–5. Explain how and why Jesus defeated the enemy and what that means to us.

4. Why is repentance so important when it comes to our being able to overcome the evil one?

5. Why is it important we reject our own pride but embrace humility?

6. Reread Galatians 5:22–23, then read the fruit of the Spirit prayer aloud to God.

7. What are strongholds and why do we need to tear them down? Study the list of strongholds and tell which ones you most relate to. Spend some time quietly praying through the prayer in the chapter to release strongholds.

8. Why is it important to rejoice in the Lord when it comes to spiritual warfare?

9. Explain why the blood of Jesus defeats the enemy. Describe how to apply the blood of Jesus in prayer. Pray a group prayer in the power of the blood of Jesus.

Chapter 6: Praying Against the Spirit of Strife

1. Read Matthew 22:37–40 and explain why we should live in a spirit of love. What would happen if more people applied the Love Principle to their lives? Can you think of new ways to apply the Love Principle to your life? If so, please share your ideas with the group.

2. How should we react to criticism? Should we always follow or always reject it? Why or why not?

3. Read Proverbs 15:1. Think of the story of Marcia then discuss the best way to handle fear in your relationships.

4. Read 2 Timothy 3:1–5. What does this Scripture mean in today's times?

5. Review the Pastor William example and discuss when and how to confront someone.

6. Is it okay to warn others when someone is dishonest or hurtful? If you were cheated by a friend, what could you say, in a godly manner, to keep someone else from being cheated by that same friend? Give a few practice examples of your warning, then agree on the best, most godly warning.

7. Quietly re-pray the body-bag prayer. If you need prayer to help you have the strength to pray this prayer, let your friends know so that they can pray for you until you are ready. If someone indicates they need prayer in this area, stop and pray for them.

8. Pray the prayer experience prayer aloud as a group.

Chapter 7: Praying for Breakthroughs

1. Discuss the definition of faith and how to apply faith to your circumstances.

2. What should we do when we are waiting on God to answer a prayer? What are six ways we can acknowledge God in our lives? Discuss the way you most want to work toward.

3. Read Philippians 3:12–14, then discuss what you think God accomplished in his people when it took them forty years to cross the desert to the Promised Land.

4. Read Luke 18:2–8 and discuss how this parable of Jesus applies to us today.

5. Think of the widow and the jars of oil. Discuss what you need to pour out of your life and discuss what God wants to pour back into your life. Create a brief prayer of invitation, inviting God to pour the things you need into your life.

6. How did Linda get her breakthrough? Can you describe breakthroughs you've encountered in your own life? Share this breakthrough with the group.

7. Pray Psalm 70 aloud.

8. Quietly pray the Prayer Experience prayer at the end of the chapter. If you wish, share your heart with the group after the prayer.

Chapter 8: Praying the Prayer of Trust

1. Linda tells of a sales expert who taught we should program our minds to get what we want from the universe. What about this teaching is off track and why? Give better examples of how we should seek a goal. Give an example of how we can turn a goal into a prayer request.

2. Why do we need to submit our goals and dreams to God? Please read the prayer listed in the chapter to do so aloud.

3. What should we do when our breakthrough has encountered a roadblock? What are roadblocks about? How should we pray when a roadblock stops our journey?

4. What happened to the woman who willfully chose to go against God and marry a man she knew was not God's best for her? What did she learn? What do you learn from her story?

5. Talk about Linda's zip-line experience. How is trusting God like jumping off a cliff? Read Psalm 23. Now read Linda's paraphrased version.

6. Read Isaiah 55:8–9. Discuss why our thoughts and ways are not always the same as God's. How do we get more in tune with God's thoughts and ways?

7. How was it that Gracie's job loss showed her God's love?

8. Why does God make us wait on an answer to prayer? Quietly, pray the prayer of waiting on God.

9. God can use a painful circumstance and turn it into a blessing. How did God use Linda's painful circumstances of getting expelled and fired? Do you think God can use your

painful circumstances? Together, ask God to turn your painful situations into a miracle.

Chapter 9: Praying Prayers of Grace and Favor

1. Discuss the difference between mercy and grace.
2. What is favor and what is the difference between winning it from God and winning it from people? Which one should we seek and why?
3. Linda says, "Only through Christ can one die but live, be beaten down but continue on, have joy through their sorrows and be rich without wealth." How can this be true? Can you give personal examples?
4. Read the list of God's promises, then look up each reference and read the promise aloud. Decide which promise is your favorite.
5. Reread Alex Kendrick's tips on finding God's favor. Discuss ways to apply these tips to your own life.
6. List the sins that hinder God's favor and discuss the one you need to work on.
7. How were the people of Israel hindered by fear? How can we avoid this same hindrance?
8. Read Psalm 34 in the Trip to the Oasis as well as the prayer in the Prayer Experience together as a prayer.

Chapter 10: Praying for Hope and Healing

1. What did Linda learn when God did not change her daughter's disabilities?
2. What lesson can we learn from God hiding Moses in a rock as he passed by?
3. Think about Elijah and his unfulfilled vision of revival and answer this question: How can the vision of what we want

from God interfere with what God wants from us? How should we respond to God regarding our dreams?

4. Discuss the three best ways to find hope and explain why you think they can help.

5. Share your favorite hope Scripture from the list of hope Scriptures and explain what the Scripture means to you.

6. Read aloud the list of affirmations based on the list of hope Scriptures. Come up with ways to apply these affirmations to your life.

7. If you need healing, ask for prayer. Then pray for healing for your group members with joy.

8. Discuss Laura's healing secret when it came to Terry's concern about amputees.

Chapter 11: The Peace That Passes Understanding

1. Read Matthew 14:22–30. Discuss how we should follow Peter's example when we are hit by the storms of life.

2. How is it that the presence of Jesus calms the storms?

3. What do you think Jesus meant when he told us that the kingdom of God is within us (Luke 17:21) as quoted in Chapter 11?

4. Review the four steps Murray says are needed to have more of the Spirit of God in our lives. Pray through these steps as a group.

5. Pray the "Have Faith That God Is with You" prayer aloud, as a group.

6. What are the three ways to leave God out of your circumstances? What can you do to invite him back into your circumstances? How can God still use your circumstances if you've messed up?

7. Will God give you peace in your storm? What should you pray to ask for that peace?

8. Pray the Trip to the Oasis prayer and the Prayer Experience prayer aloud as a group.

Chapter 12: Find Real Joy

1. Read Mark 8:31–33 and discuss what happens when we seek God's favor over seeking God.
2. Linda says you are going to get a miracle whether God changes your circumstances or changes you. What do you think she means by that?
3. Review Shepherd's Hierarchy of Faith and discuss where you think you were when you started this book and where you think you are now.
4. What are the four things that happen when we abide with Christ? Give an example of what each of these things might "look" like.
5. Read Deuteronomy 33:27 and discuss how this verse fits with Linda's example about carrying her sleeping son through the mall.
6. How can we rest in God when we have a difficult decision to make?
7. Shadrach, Meshach, and Abednego refused to worship Nebuchadnezzar's false god and were tossed into a fiery furnace, yet not a hair on their heads was singed. Why not? What can we do to duplicate Christ's presence in our own fiery trials?
8. Read 1 Thessalonians 5:16–18 and describe how we can apply these concepts to our problems such as bitterness and pain, jealousy and envy, anger and strife, discontentment, worry, fear, and disappointment.
9. Read Psalm 100:1–5 and the Prayer Experience as a group prayer.

Notes

Chapter 1 When Difficulties Come

1. Billy Graham, http://www.brainyquote.com/quotes/authors/b/billy_graham.html.

2. Dr. David Jeremiah, *Turning Point*, June 18, 2009, http://www.oneplace.com.

3. Dr. Norman Vincent Peale, http://www.worldofquotes.com/topic/trouble/index.html.

Chapter 2 Finding God in Your Circumstances

1. Andrew Murray, *How to Strengthen Your Faith* (New Kensington, PA: Whittaker House, 1997), 75.

2. Ibid., 74.

3. Leslie Vernick, *How to Find Selfless Joy in a Me-First World* (Colorado Springs, CO: WaterBrook Press, 2003), 21.

4. Anne Graham Lotz, *I Saw the Lord* (Grand Rapids: Zondervan, 2006), 79–80.

Chapter 3 Five Keys to Surviving Difficult Times

1. Andrew Murray, *Absolute Surrender* (Bloomington, MN: Bethany House, 1985, 2003), 144.

2. John Wesley, http://thinkexist.com/quotation/do_all_the_good_you_can-by_all_the_means_you_can/148152.html.

3. David Wilkerson, *The Vision and Beyond* (World Challenge Publications, 2003), 49–50.

4. Murray, *Absolute Surrender*, 75.

Chapter 4 Giving Your Troubles to God

1. Billy Graham, http://www.brainyquote.com/quotes/authors/b/billy_graham_2.html.

2. Dr. J. Vernon McGee, *Edited Messages on Job*, http://www.oneplace.com/Ministries/Thru_the_Bible_with_JVernon_McGee/Article.asp?article_id=1774.

3. Noah's name definition, Biblesoft's New Exhaustive Strong's Numbers and Concordance with Expanded Greek-Hebrew Dictionary (Biblesoft and International Bible Translators, 1994).

Chapter 5 Standing Against the Darkness

1. Francis Frangipane, *The Three Battlegrounds* (Cedar Rapids, IA: Arrow Publications, 1989, 2006), 59.

2. www.dictionary.com.

3. Ibid.

4. Frangipane, *The Three Battlegrounds*, 43.

5. Ibid., 53.

6. Ibid., 51.

Chapter 6 Praying Against the Spirit of Strife

1. Max Lucado, *Hope Pure and Simple: 316 Thoughts to Lift Your Soul* (Nashville: Thomas Nelson, 2007), 81.

2. Charles R. Swindoll, http://thinkexist.com/quotes/charles_r._swindoll/2.html.

3. Patsy Clairmont, *Dancing Bones* (Nashville: Thomas Nelson, 2007), 172.

4. Lucado, *Hope Pure and Simple*, 28.

Chapter 7 Praying for Breakthroughs

1. Francis Frangipane, *The Power of Covenant Prayer* (Lake Mary, FL: Creation House, 1998), 123.

2. Ibid., 139.

3. Arnold Henry Glasow, http://www.coolquotes.com/trouble.html.

4. Adoniram Judson, in Nick Harrison, *Magnificent Prayer* (Grand Rapids: Zondervan, 2001), 241.

Chapter 8 Praying the Prayer of Trust

1. E. M. Bounds, http://www.famousquotesandauthors.com/authors/e__m__bounds_quotes.html.

2. Max Lucado, http://www.goodreads.com/quotes/show/14109.

3. C. S. Lewis, http://www.brainyquote.com/quotes/authors/c/c_s_lewis_2.html.

4. Margaret Feinberg, *The Sacred Echo* (Grand Rapids: Zondervan, 2008), 38.

5. E. M. Bounds, http://www.famousquotesandauthors.com/authors/e__m__bounds_quotes.html.

6. Ibid.

Chapter 9 Praying Prayers of Grace and Favor

1. www.dictionary.com.
2. Ibid.
3. http://www.bigsiteofamazingfacts.com/when-did-president-ulysses-s-grant-walk-on-silver-bricks.
4. Alex Kendrick, www.IgniteMyFaith.com.
5. Lotz, *I Saw the Lord*, 178–79.

Chapter 10 Praying for Hope and Healing

1. Charles Swindoll, http://thinkexist.com/quotes/charles_r._swindoll/.

Chapter 11 The Peace That Passes Understanding

1. C. S. Lewis, http://www.brainyquote.com/quotes/authors/c/c_s_lewis.html.
2. Tornado verification, http://rammb.cira.colostate.edu/visit/blog/index.php/2008/05/30/the-weld-county-colorado-tornadoes-of-may-22-2008/.
3. Kay Arthur, Oneplace.com, April 15, 2007, http://www.oneplace.com/Ministries/Precept/Article.asp?article_id=1469.
4. Andrew Murray, *Absolute Surrender*, 29–30.
5. Ibid.
6. Ibid.
7. Ibid.
8. Ibid.
9. Ibid.
10. Ibid.
11. Ibid.
12. *True Miracles*, www.IgniteMyFaith.com.

Chapter 12 Find Real Joy

1. Neil T. Anderson, http://protestantism.suite101.com/article.cfm/great_quotes_for_christians_on_trusting_god.
2. Rick Warren, http://www.beliefnet.com/Faiths/Christianity/2009/01/Christian-Quotes-About-God-and-Love.aspx?p=4.
3. Feinberg, *The Sacred Echo*, 125.

Linda Evans Shepherd is the author of more than thirty books, including *When You Don't Know What to Pray: How to Talk to God about Anything* and the bestselling novel series the Potluck Club and the Potluck Catering Club, written with Eva Marie Everson.

An internationally recognized speaker, Linda has spoken in almost every state in the country and around the world. You can learn more about her speaking ministry at www.RefreshingSpeaker.com.

Linda is also a media personality and a frequent television host of *Denver Celebration*. She hosts several online TV programs such as *Cooking Up Wonders* as seen on www.RightToTheHeart.tv.

Linda is the president of Right to the Heart Ministries. She is the CEO of AWSA (Advanced Writers and Speakers Association), which ministers to Christian authors and speakers. To learn more about Linda's ministries, go to: www.VisitLinda.com.

Linda has been married to Paul for thirty-plus years and is the mother of two children.

To find more information about this book, go to www.Ignite MyFaith.com.

Or use your smart phone to visit the website using the QR code below:

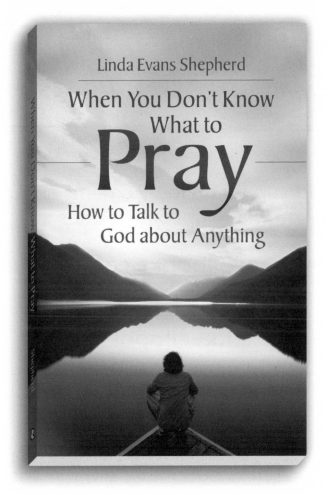